COUNTRY LIV

THE
Country Look

COUNTRY LIVING

THE Country Look
AND HOW TO GET IT

Text by
Mary Seehafer Sears

Foreword by
Rachel Newman

HEARST BOOKS
New York

Library of Congress Cataloging-in-Publication Data

Country living magazine
Country living, Country look/text by Mary Seehafer Sears; foreword by Rachel Newman.
p. cm.
ISBN 0-688-09358-2 (hc), 1-58816-007-6 (pb)
1. Handicraft—United States.   2. Interior decoration—United States. I. Sears, Mary Seehafer.   II. Title.
TT157.S37   1991
745—dc20

90-22492
CIP

Printed in Singapore

First Paperback Edition 2001
1 2 3 4 5 6 7 8 9 10

Front cover photograph by Keith Scott Morton
Back cover photographs (top to bottom left) by Joshua Green, Paul Nystrom and Keith Scott Morton and (top to bottom right) by André Gillardin, Jessie Walker and Jessie Walker.

Produced by Smallwood and Stewart, Inc., New York

Edited by Susan E. Davis
Design by Dirk Kaufman
Illustrations by Julie Ridenour and Suzanne Lincoln
Project directions by Eleanor Levie and Jennifer Place

www.countryliving.com

CONTENTS

Painted
Effects 110

Built
by Hand 164

Resources
188

Photography Credits
190

Foreword

With profound pleasure, *Country Living* presents *Country Living's Country Look*. Its publication forges new ground for us. For the first time, we are presenting crafts projects in tandem with a huge portfolio of decorating ideas. Clear and easy how-to instructions are interspersed with hundreds of pictures of beautiful country homes, many of them photographed in detail. Instead of merely admiring a look, you'll be able to recreate it. Choosing your favorite projects—the ones that suit your own unique talents—will help you fashion your personal country environment.

A popular Shaker motto extols the virtues of putting hands to work. We think this book fits the bill. *Country Living's Country Look* was born in answer to many readers' requests. Over the years we have heard from many country aficionados who are eager to "do it themselves." They want to build, paint, stitch, and stencil. *Country Living's Country Look* provides the instruction that can turn these dreams into reality. *Country Living* magazine's furniture projects have always been a popular feature. *Country Living's Country Look* broadens the how-to concept to embrace an even wider range of craftspeople. Whether you're a collector, a seamstress, or an artist with paint or wood, there are projects here for you.

On a personal level, this book pleases me very much. My father was an artist, so working with hands and heart on dearly beloved projects is a familiar ritual for me. My own greatest relaxation comes when I am curled up with my knitting or needlepoint. The decoration in my office include a needlepoint pillow and pottery I made myself. There are also framed bits of lace and a cherished pair of hand-crocheted gloves, now a bit yellowed with age. I like to think they were probably worn by a long-ago lady at a tea dance or country cakewalk.

When *Country Living* magazine first began touting the country look in 1978, our work was underscored by the steadfast belief that people craved warm, reassuring places to live. Not for us the sleek chrome and glass that was so popular at the time. Instead, we believed in the home as nest, filled with bits and pieces gathered here and there. Just as a bird gathers bits of cotton and sticks for a nest, so the country dweller fashions the home.

So the long life of the "country look" comes as no suprise. In truth, it is a way of life that has endured for generations. Time has simply added a richer patina to the objects and items we have accumulated.

Rachel Newman

Founding Editor
Country Living

Introduction

We all know the country look has changed over the years. Yet its essence remains strong and true. Whether a home is on a rural lane or a bustling crosstown street, country is a state of mind. It's a way of life that goes on developing, just as America has.

More than 300 years have passed since the first pioneers set up housekeeping on American soil. But people are still nesting in down-to-earth houses set up for practical living. And they're decorating them country-style, with all kinds of variations on that theme.

The rituals of hearth and home continue: apples in a yellowware bowl, fair linen cloths shaken out and then slid atop well-scrubbed tables, crazy quilts on old brass beds, a fire in the fireplace. There is so much to enjoy about continued traditions rich with history and nostalgia. Creating the country look is a way of carrying on these traditions.

Can anyone pass a tumbled-down house without wondering what's inside? Who hasn't experienced the thrill of the auction, antiques shop, flea market, even the neighborhood garage sale?

Even garbage days are fair game for the true country addict. Who knows what can be found? The possibilities include everything from a huge carved headboard, to wicker baskets, to windowboxes for the geraniums. These are the finds—treasures with a past. They make their way from home to home, like the itinerant artists of yesteryear, bringing new kinds of joy and fulfilling new uses each time they cross another threshold.

Country Living's Country Look is another in the series of books published under the aegis of *Country Living* magazine. Devoted to a combination of decorating and crafts, the book is a sampler of ideas on how to give a house that special country flavor. Imagination abounds here. Besides a wealth of photographs and descriptive text, each chapter includes how-to instructions for making things. That means the pictures can become reality in any house.

In order to represent the most popular country crafts and categories, we sliced the book into quarters.

For ideas on giving a house that overall festive, lived-in mood, start right in with the first chap-

ter, The Country Style. It spotlights all the essential minutiae that, collectively, express country. Hats, dried flowers, wreaths, and various and sundry collections—they're all here. These ideas are worthy of copying, like the projects on drying flowers for bouquets and herbs for potpourris and on making a pinecone wreath. Just remember that more than one of anything is a collection. Displaying things with a flair is the key.

The next chapter, Decorating with Fabrics, is probably the juiciest section of *Country Living's Country Look*—which isn't suprising, considering how many country things are spun, woven, or embellished with thread. There are pages and pages filled with exquisite needlework, treasured quilts, and braided and hooked rugs. Beautiful photographs of old and new samplers, imaginative window treatments, and handmade floor-coverings, as well as thirteen projects, including turkeywork, bed hangings, and tiebacks, may start you on a few new hobbies.

The third chapter, Painted Effects, sounds like a category in the Academy Awards—and in a way, it is. This part of the book is devoted to transformations—the kind that takes place with paint and some Early American "helpers" like feathers, combs, rags, stencils, and brushes. The painting techniques showcased here, including two projects on faux finishes and three on stenciling, have remained in favor through the centuries and promise to give any room a time-honored appearance.

The last chapter, Built by Hand, speaks to anyone who has a streak of craftsmanship in his or her blood. If weaving a chair seat or building a bird house or a gameboard is appealing, here's the chance. Someone once said the person who can sew can be a carpenter. What better place to start than with these noble country pastimes?

Country Living's Country Look also spotlights present-day craftspeople: a potter, a stenciler, a muralist, a rugmaker, a tinsmith, and a woodworker. These artisans are the jewels of the book. Each one is carrying on a rich tradition, working by hand. They follow in the footsteps of the men, women, and children who helped shape this country's artistic heritage in centuries past.

May this book offer encouragement and inspiration, so you can put together your own country look, your own way.

Mary Seehafer Sears

The Country Style

That Country Warmth

People who long to create the country look in their homes have only to see authentic country homes to be inspired. Yet, what surprises some people is that the decorating effects we prize today have their origins in humble sources.

In the early farmhouses of America, practicality was paramount. The home was arranged primarily for utility, not for show. Plucking a basket from a ceiling beam was a convenient way to gather the day's garden crops. Drying herbs to be put away for the colder months was a seasonal ritual. Homespun woven by the evening fire covered the windows, and rag rugs fashioned from outgrown or old clothes softened the floors. In the kitchen, pots were hung close at hand. And in Shaker homes, sweeping was easy because the chairs were hung on the wall.

Today, nostalgia for days gone by has sent many of us scurrying back to this simple country style. And if we haven't actually moved to the country, we are nonetheless able to fill our houses with the objects and effects that bring that notion to life.

Busy, lived-in rooms have a magnetism that's difficult to pinpoint but simple to sense. In these rooms, it's easy to pull up a chair, have a talk, and keep an eye on the kids at the same time. The lighting's just right, something pleasing decorates the wall, the view may be soothing, too. And invariably, the room says something about the family who lives there. There's a blanket tucked on the arm of the wing chair because it gets chilly at night. There's an ottoman nearby, a basket full of magazines, maybe even a jigsaw puzzle strewn across the table. The pillows on the sofa may have been stitched from old quilt pieces, and the hand-hooked rug by the fire might feature the family pet. A pile of seasoned logs waits by the fire.

This is the kind of house that welcomes from the drive. Flowers border the driveway, a basket of geraniums waits at the door. Bunnies nest beneath the bushes; real or ceramic, they are charming just the same. The toys scattered about the lawn hint at the larger life within.

Of course, a country home is more than just objects. It's scents and sights as well: vanilla candles burning in tin sconces, an herb wreath as a centerpiece on the table, cups of tea with sprigs of fresh mint, homemade cranberry nut muffins in a basket.

Yet, putting together a true country home has more to do with real life than with gathering props. People dry herbs and hang them on kitchen pegs because they like to grow them in their gardens and cook with them. The collection of miniature ships on someone's library shelves hints at his maritime hobbies. These days, the woman who keeps a spinning wheel on her hearth is usually an honest-to-goodness weaver.

A country house is proud of its heritage and of its owners' way of life. That's the most important part of what makes it appealing.

This farmhouse built in 1983 has many of the hallmarks of a Colonial dwelling. In the dining room, sunbonnets, aprons, dried flowers, baskets, and candles dangle from the peg racks. More baskets hang from the overhead beams, which were stained to match the wide pine floorboards. Stoneware marches in an orderly row beneath a 24-pane window decorated with cheerful tin cutouts.

Hats on the Wall

Hats command attention. Whether they're perched on someone's head or hung on a wall, they tend to provoke comment or at least curiosity. The attraction is different, though: a person who wears a hat has an air of being in charge, while a room decorated with hats conveys an old-fashioned, sentimental air. There's something about trailing ribbons, garlands of flowers, and the texture and scent of straw or wool that conjures up images of leisurely pursuits. Picnics, boating on a lake, games of croquet played on the lawn on a midsummer's day, and sipping lemonade at an afternoon tea party all demand a hat. And a room decorated with an eye to the past calls for hats as well.

Hats have history. Some people collect hats everywhere they go: this one worn at a Western rodeo, that one purchased at a Kentucky crafts fair. Sometimes a flea-market trunk yields up a passel of old-fashioned hats wrapped in crumbling tissue paper. From these chance beginnings, a decorating tool emerges.

Hanging hats requires no more than a daring imagination; any room can potentially benefit from the addition of a hat. A peg rack or freestanding coat rack is the most logical place to hang hats. Other imaginative souls have hung hats on window frames or across kitchen soffitts or have placed them at ceiling height to create a frieze around a room.

Hats are perhaps most often displayed in the more intimate areas of the house—a bedroom, dressing area, or bath—but they are equally suitable in other, more public rooms like the living or dining room or foyer. In fact, displaying hats in an entry makes perfect sense. One can always grab a hat from a display and sail off, confident that her public impression will have punch because she's wearing a hat.

When they're not being worn, hats often end up decorating bedrooms: clustered with mirrors, paintings, and drawings (above left); just an arm's length away from the dresser (above right); and clustered along one wall in an informal assemblage (right). A collection of whimsical and wearable toppers (opposite) evokes a playful mood, perched on pegs embedded in an exposed brick wall in a landmark Manhattan townhouse.

Collections on Parade

Every collection, however grand, starts with just one piece. Anytime there are two of something, a collection is underway. And collections, whatever their nature, are one of the mainstays of the country look. Displaying collections, whatever their nature or size, is an easy way to give a country feeling to a house.

Glance around a single room and there are all kinds of nooks and crannies where collections can roost. Shelves are the most obvious place. Bowls look great marching across them—the better to see their pretty designs. Everyone leans plates against the backs of cupboard shelves for the same reason. Windowsills cry out for collections, and so do the window sashes and tiny ledges formed by the molding at the tops of windows. A stairway or even a floor can serve as a roosting place for a collection of doorstops, tiny wooden animals, bears sipping from a miniature tea set. It's easy, once you get the idea.

Collections need not be expensive, precious, or antique. Everyday platters, salt and pepper shakers, and baskets are worthy of display. Old books can be grouped together with old family portraits for a yesteryear effect. Color is also a way of tying a collection together. Disparate objects, all blue and white, can be the basis of an intriguing display.

The best collections show their owners' interests and give a home a personal look. That's country decorating at its very best.

An assortment of bale-handle boxes, salt-glazed pottery, cookie cutters, yellowware, and lady-apple pomanders stocks the shelves of a Florida buttery (above). Local finds—including ovoid salt-glazed jugs, period butter molds, and pantry boxes—are lovingly displayed in a kitchen in central Wisconsin (opposite). Hand-dipped candles decorate the quilt rack. A rag doll gets a bird's-eye view from atop a row of Indian baskets. The frieze was achieved by airbrushing acrylics on hand-cut stencils.

Open shelves in a kitchen (left) are the ideal place to show off a neatly arranged assortment of white ironstone plates and pitchers, pretty teacups, the fetching labels of imported oils, teas and jams, and dainty black-and-white "treasures." New renditions of curvy Thirties pitchers line the countertop. A more rugged, random collection huddles in an open country cupboard (opposite). Woodenware is stacked among clusters of brambles, dried flowers, and branches, with an abandoned bird's nest with eggs the focal point.

A *sweep of open shelves (above) shows off Meyer pottery, an indigenous Texas treasure. The collection includes early salt-glazed pots, slip-glazed items, and souvenir ware. Some collections are made to be used. This dining room table (right) is set with new slip-decorated redware made with nontoxic glazes that is safe to eat from. The cupboard is filled with New England–style slipware. A rural Missouri couple's collection of period collectibles is displayed in the kitchen of a restored 1920s guesthouse (opposite above). Fiesta ware and jadeite canisters brighten the old oak cupboard and Detroit Jewel cookstove. Removing kitchen cupboard doors (opposite below) leaves special dishes on view and close at hand.*

A Master of the Wheel

Ned Foltz is a redware potter in Lancaster County, Pennsylvania. His work carries on a folk tradition begun more than 200 years ago by early German settlers, who found the soil and setting conducive to making earthenware.

Growing up in Lancaster County with artistic talent and a grandmother in the antiques business piqued Ned's interest in old redware pottery. He started collecting it when he was 15 years old.

After graduating from art school, Foltz returned to Lancaster County to teach art in a public school. While living on a rented farm one summer, Foltz decided to try his hand at making redware pottery. His first attempts were pie plates, unglazed inkwells, and candle holders fired in the farm's old furnace. Soon shops began to buy his wares, and Foltz took up potting full time.

Foltz's shop is a restored 1830 one-room schoolhouse with thick stone walls and a distinctive red-clay tile roof—made by Foltz, of course. Foltz and his wife, Gwen, live in an old gristmill up the road.

Foltz digs Pennsylvania red clay from the ground and mixes it with a commercial clay that has more plasticity.

The resulting ware is sturdier than the kind Pennsylvania's early potters were able to make. Foltz fashions all the hand-turned circular redware himself using a potter's wheel. Using Foltz's designs, his assistant works with the slab method, rolling out the clay and shaping rectangular pieces over a form. Gwen, an artist who does all Ned's color work, decorates the slipware with liquid yellow clay poured on to the red-clay base with a slip cup. Other pieces are scratch-decorated using the sgraffito technique—the design is cut into slip-coated clay to expose the red clay beneath.

Potter Ned Foltz (above) decorates a redware vase with clay leaves; he impresses them with the veins of real leaves. Earthenware distributes heat evenly, so the hand-turned plates (opposite top) are perfect for baking pies. They were coated with yellow slip and stenciled with several colors using a sponge. A platter with a free-hand bird-and-flower motif (opposite below right) was decorated using the sgraffito technique. Heart-shaped redware dishes (opposite below left) are hand-formed and decorated with sculptured leaves, flowers, and grapes. Clay stamps make the inner surfaces more decorative.

A simple, but engaging way to perk up a room during the summer months is to pick a bouquet of garden flowers and place them in a row of blue bottles on a windowsill (above). Bouquets of dried wild flowers (opposite) have traditionally been used to adorn walls, both outside and inside the house. A festive display of dried flowers dresses up a porch, while a basket with live flowers on the floor adds an exciting counterpoint.

Potpourri, Dried Flowers, and Herbs

Flowers are the essence of springtime and summer, and fall's farewell. Drying flowers captures their heady scent and fragile beauty. Then they can be enjoyed in the house year round, in bundles and bouquets or as fragrant potpourri.

Some dried flowers keep their original look and color. Other flowers wither a bit and take on a dustier hue reminiscent of an aged sepia photograph. Herbs and decorative grasses can also be cut and dried in much the same way as flowers.

Chive blossoms and bay leaves enhance herbal mixtures (below left). Potpourri nestles in romantic hand-painted boxes, both oval and heart-shaped

(below right). The fresh-cut pickings from a Los Angeles garden (opposite) will soon be dried and blended into fragrant potpourri.

If one is sentimental, saving bouquets or single roses holds great appeal. After the flowers have dried, just nest them in tissue paper or tie the stems with bows of narrow ribbon to create a romantic mood.

The drying process is easy (see the dried flower project on page 34). In fact, the plants look quite attractive scattered about on open screen trays or hanging from the ceiling as they dry; that way it's easy to monitor the procedure from start to finish.

Because it is dark and airy, an attic or garage is often the best place for drying flowers and herbs. Sometimes a dark hallway close to the garden fits the bill. Dried flowers lend themselves to hanging. They are often displayed in bundles upside down, just as they were hung to dry. A Shaker peg rack or simple hooks can hold dried flowers and herbs in any room of the house. Or the flowers may simply be

bundled and arranged en masse: above a bathroom mirror or crowning a doorway, for example.

On a grander scale, there's nothing more dramatic than bunches of dried flowers and herbs which hang from the ceiling. A barn, garage, raftered family room, or crafts shed is perfect for this kind of effect. On a screened-in or open-air porch, a ceiling full of dried flowers and herbs catches the breeze and sends out a pleasant scent.

Different kinds of containers make interesting vessels for dried flower bouquets. Dried baby's breath looks wonderful massed in huge baskets. Mounds of hydrangeas are dramatic in large pantry boxes. Lavendar and statice are charming tucked in white china vases. The combinations are endless.

Potpourri made from dried flower petals, spices, and essential oils is a scented surprise inside a covered container. A tiny hatbox is an ideal hiding place for potpourri. Potpourri can also be a tactile delight when spread out in a shallow dish or decorative plate. Occasionally, scattering the top of dried potpourri with some fresh-picked flower heads gives the mixture a fresh look.

No kitchen should be without its bundles of fresh garden herbs, cut and dried anytime from August until the first frost in fall. Positioned close to the stove, dried herbs can be easily snipped and added to a bubbling pot as culinary inspiration strikes. In the pantry, an orderly row of dried herbs hung from nails close to mixing bowls serves the same purpose and is pretty besides.

Instead of hats, bunches of dried statice hang from the pegs of an old whitewashed hat rack on a Florida porch (right). The dry sink, newly made to look old, bears other gifts from the garden. Part of a Victorian dining room in upstate New York (opposite far left) is devoted to making bouquets of everlastings and fragrant potpourris. The preserved blooms, herbs, grains, cattails, and raffia extend the joys of gardening through the year. The still life (opposite above right) is composed of a graduating line of chive-blossom bouquets lashed to a handmade twig drying rack. A punctuating bouquet of dried flowers hangs above a basket found in southern France. A dowel suspended from the mantelpiece of a walk-in stone fireplace (opposite below right) is an impromptu drying rack for bouquets of garden flowers.

Dried Flowers and Potpourri

The earliest published mention of drying flowers was in 1594 by Sir Hugh Platt in *Delights for Ladies*, where he described drying roses, pansies, and stock gillyflowers in layers of sand.

Victorian parlors were often enhanced by a "winter bouquet" made of dried flowers, herbs, and leaves. Meaning was attached to different ones—basil, for example, represented love—so tiny arrangements were often given as gifts. Wedding bouquets were preserved by covering each petal with paraffin.

Techniques for drying flowers have changed little from Victorian times. Flowers are dried by letting them hang upside down in bunches in a dark, dry, well-ventilated room or by layering them in silica gel or borax. Now herbs can be dried in a microwave.

The key to arranging your dried flowers is imagination. Try tying bundles of flowers with thick twine or vines. Combine them with seasonal fruit or fresh vegetables. Scour flea markets or shops for unusual containers.

DIRECTIONS

CHOOSING FLOWERS: On a warm, sunny day, pick the most perfect-looking blooms at the peak of their maturity. Make sure any morning dew or rain has evaporated, so the flowers are as dry as possible. If there is moisture in the flower heads, allow the stemmed flowers to stand in 2"-3" (5-8 cm) of warm water until the heads are completely dry. Since flowers may shrink, fade, or fall apart with any drying method, pick more than twice as many as you think you will need. Drying times will vary from days to weeks, depending on the flower and the drying environment. Whatever drying method you use, wait until the leaves and petals are as dry as paper and the stems snap apart when they are bent.

HANG DRYING: Works well for flowers with twiggy stalks and small heads such as everlastings, statice, baby's breath, lavender, clover, tea roses, bachelor's buttons, Chinese lanterns, hydrangeas, and most herbs. Choose a dry, dark, warm, well-ventilated place. Attics are often the best drying areas. You can experiment with drying places by hanging flowers of the same type in different spots at the same time and then comparing drying times and color retention.

Strip the first few inches of leaves off the stems. Tie the flowers together in small bunches with cotton string, leaving the string ends long. Fasten these ends to a peg, nail, rafter, clothesline, or other support, so that air can circulate all around the flowers.

FLAT DRYING: Works well for drying potpourri ingredients: orange and lemon peel, fragrant grasses, eucalyptus, myrtle, and herbs such as basil, bay, lemon balm, rose geranium, rosemary, tarragon, and thyme; works for full-blown flowers such as roses, peonies, and dahlias, but they do not retain their shape and color. Place the flowers on window screening supported on blocks so that air may circulate under as well as around them. Turn the flowers every other day. You could also use a coarse mesh (such as hardware cloth), slipping the stems through the mesh so that one side of the flower head does not get flattened.

USING SILICA GEL OR BORAX METHOD: Best preserves shapes and colors but not scents for large, delicate-petaled flowers; works well for roses, chrysanthemums, daisies, carnations, marigolds, pansies. Crushed silica gel is available from craft and florist's supply shops; follow the directions that come with it.

Begin by pouring a 2" (5.1-cm) layer of silica gel or borax in a large plaster box. Carefully strip or cut the leaves from the stems. Cut off the stem about 2"–3" from the

flower head. If desired, you can dry leaves and stems, but do them separately. Place each flower face down in the silica gel or borax, making sure the flowers do not touch one another. Pour more grains carefully around and over the flowers until they are completely covered. Allow some grains to lie between the petals to support them and to help the flower retain its shape. Place a test flower in each box, inserting a little marker to help you locate this bloom. Keep checking this test flower until its texture is like taffeta; then remove the rest of the flowers.

To remove the flowers, insert a spatula under the flower head and work the flower out carefully. Use a watercolor brush to remove any grains that cling to the petals.

QUICK DRYING: Works well for scented leaves such as geraniums (available in lemon, orange, peppermint, vanilla, and even chocolate fragrances), mint, rosemary, bay laurel, sage, and thyme. Spread leaves on a cheesecloth-covered rack or baking sheet in a 90°F oven. Leave the door open and stir the leaves occasionally. For most herbs, you may use a microwave: Thick leaves take up to 3 minutes; smaller, drier leaves should be done in 1 minute.

FINISHING FOR ARRANGEMENTS: To protect dried flowers for arranging, stick their stems temporarily in a piece of plastic foam so that they remain standing. Working in a well-ventilated area, spray the flowers with several light coats of clear acrylic and let them dry.

MAKING POTPOURRI: Use 4 cups of partially dried petals such as roses, camomile, violets, lilac, honeysuckle, lilies of the valley, carnations, nasturtium, and white jasmine. (Partially dried flowers and petals best absorb and retain scented oils.)

Add 1 tablespoon of herbs or spices such as allspice, clove, cinnamon, or any herb listed in Flat Drying.

Add ⅓ cup powdered fixative, such as orrisroot, and 3 drops of essential oil, both available at craft and florist's supply shops. Add citrus peel or a little cologne or brandy. (You can also use these ingredients to revitalize an old or tired potpourri.)

Mix everything together and place it in airtight jars. Let the mixture stand for four weeks, stirring once or twice each week.

To retain the scent, keep the potpourri in a covered container and open the lid only when you wish to release the scent. If the potpourri is to be displayed in an open container, add a few thoroughly dried flower heads for color and texture.

The Endless Variety of Wreaths

For instant cheer, hang a wreath. This symbol of continuity and constancy can brighten any space. Wreaths look glorious on doors, of course. What would Christmas be without them? An oversized wreath makes a bold statement over a fireplace or at the peak of a roof. A wreath can be a natural window dressing—sometimes taking the place of a valance or curtains. Little wreaths have a charm all their own, especially when embellished with bows of baby ribbons.

Wreaths can be made from almost anything. They are traditionally fashioned from natural materials like holly, grapevines, pine boughs, and pinecones. (See the cone wreath project on page 38.) Herb wreaths, which give off a constant fragrance, can be refreshing. A lavender wreath, for instance, holds its scent for months and is a delicate bedroom decoration as well.

Grapevine wreaths on salvaged shed shutters enclose a bathtub in a restored nineteenth-century log house (above right), while a tangle of bittersweet encircles the chandelier. An unfinished picket fence in Florida is graced with a grapevine wreath, as is the welcoming cement angel by the open porch door (right). Large and small wreaths frame the view from the window of a California cottage (opposite). Twining the same dried flowers over the beams continues the theme overhead.

A Pinecone Wreath

The traditional pinecone wreath is a popular, decorative addition to a door or wall. Wreaths can be stark and simple or profusely elaborate. This project shows how to make a basic wreath, but think about customizing these instructions according to the season or the occasion. For example, just add nuts or berries, or spray paint pinecones silver, gold, or other colors. Use miniature gourds and seedpods at Thanksgiving, and add tiny colored lights or balls at Christmas. Attach bits of antique valentines, flowers and lace to the wreath, or even photographs. Apply colorful ribbons, beads, and other embellishments. If the wreath is for a boy's room, attach miniature cars and trucks; if it's for a girl's room, add tiny dolls or dollhouse furniture.

Any type of pinecone will work, but cones from the white pine tree are readily available, and the white resin that clings to the edges forms a natural illusion of snow.

DIRECTIONS

YOU WILL NEED: Dried materials gathered from the backyard or a woodland or purchased at craft stores or craft departments of good florist's shops. Gather a large assortment of dried pinecones and fir cones, plus any of the following: large seedpods, lotus pods, protea flats, chicalote chokes (greasewood), artificial crab apples (optional). Also needed are a wire wreath with 2 to 4 concentric rings, florist's wire, wire snips, a glue gun, and hot-melt glue sticks.

MAKING A HANGING RING: If your wire wreath does not have a hanging ring, make one as follows: Loosely coil florist's wire several times around an intersection of wires on the back of the wreath to form a ring. Wrap the end of the florist's wire back around itself and cut off the excess.

PREPARING CONES: If you've picked up cones from the ground, they may be partially or totally closed. To open the petals up and kill any resident insects, roast the cones on foil-covered cookie sheets in a 200°F oven for about an hour. This will also seal the sap, giving the cones a shiny coat. A word of caution: The smell from your oven may or may not be pleasantly pine-scented, so make sure the kitchen area is well-ventilated.

USING A HOT-GLUE GUN: A glue gun dispenses a hot

adhesive that bonds almost immediately. It will allow you to secure items where you want them, at any angle or point of contact. Follow the manufacturer's instructions; keep a bowl of cold water handy for accidental burns.

WIRING ITEMS: For pinecones, wrap the wire tightly around the cone between the bottom tiers of petals (those nearest the stem). For other items, wrap the stem tightly with wire; apply a dab of hot glue to secure it. Twist the wire ends together and leave them 2″ (5.1 cm) long.

ARRANGING: Place the largest items between the rings of the wreath, and wrap each wire end at least twice around a different ring. Place medium-size and smaller cones toward the inside or outside of the wreath, and bring the wire ends around the back of the ring, twisting them together to secure. Flatten the wires against the back of the wreath, and snip off any long ends.

For a well-balanced design, begin with the largest items and work toward the smallest. Work with one type and size of floral material at a time, and space each type fairly evenly all around the wreath. One exception: Save the most decorative items such as especially pretty cones and pods or apples for last, so that they will be the most visible. When the rings of the wreath are all concealed, use smaller items and decorative pieces to fill in the spaces between the larger cones and florals. Again, space them evenly all around. Hot-glue these pieces in place, wedging their stems and sides between other items but allowing their tips or flat surfaces to protrude.

Decorating with Fabrics

This old-style workroom is the domain of someone who loves to sew. The cupboard's contents become part of the decor: Colorful bolts of calico rest on the shelves, threads are draped on an open door, and skeins of yarn spill out of a lower drawer. A striped floorcloth and a woven chair seat are in keeping with the room's handcrafted flavor. (You will find directions for how to make a floorcloth on page 152 and a woven chair seat page 182.)

Fabric ~ A Softening Presence

Fabrics play an essential role in any house, and nowhere is that more apparent than in the country dwelling. Inherent in the architecture are lots of hard surfaces—plaster walls, exposed beams, stone hearths, tiled floors. All demand a softening presence, and fabrics are the answer.

One look around the house will reveal what needs help. This room could use a rug. That window needs a fresh valance. Wouldn't a quilt look nice in the foyer?

Just stepping inside a fabric store or knit shop is enough for those who work with their hands. Each spool of thread, each bolt of cotton, each skein of wool offers so many possibilities. In fact, the look of these shops hasn't changed much through the years. The colorful stacks of calicos and bins of hand-dyed wool remain the same. With a little imagination, it is easy to envision our ancestors experiencing the same anticipation and pleasure as they stood in a tiny general store or dry-goods establishment deciding what to buy.

The countrywoman's sewing kit was never far from hand. When she had time to sit (which wasn't often, unless her husband was wealthy), she could be found with needle and thread, adding to the family's wardrobe, darning socks, or embroidering bedding with colorful designs.

Sewing was one way for the Early American woman to exercise her artistry. And the needlework that survives today attests to her skills. Intricate handwork, made up of hundreds of stitches, knots, braids, and finishing touches, is one of the most personal forms of decorating. Because each creation is one of a kind, handwork expresses the creator like no other kind of work.

Quilting is another age-old craft that's being carried on today. Not only does quilting provide a respite from the day's pressures, but it is a means of expression, just as it was years ago. Quilts are still given as gifts, just as they were in centuries past.

The current renaissance of rug making should come as no surprise. With more and more country homeowners clamoring for authentic decor, artisans with a talent for recreating the past are offering fine goods for sale.

Hand-stitched linens and handmade quilts and rugs require patience and dexterity. If you're blessed with both, your home will probably bear witness to your talents. If you wish to try your hand, the many easy projects in this chapter offer a variety of items to make with fabrics. For those who like the look but are less than nimble with a needle, there are plenty of shops, mail-order catalogs, and artists and craftspeople available to help.

American and Danish samplers are examples of turn-of-the-century handiwork (left).

A collection of samplers in a variety of shapes and sizes (opposite) is arranged in a montage above the headboard of a bed.

Stitches in Time

The earliest samplers were stitched by women to record embroidery or lace patterns. In fact, the word "sampler" comes from the Latin word *exemplar*, which means "pattern." By the 1500s, samplers were "wrought" by young ladies as part of their introduction to the domestic arts. Samplers—literally, samples of their work—were worked on squares, rectangles, or strips of cotton, linen, or wool and showed a girl's full repertoire of stitches executed in colorful silk or cotton threads. After that, whenever something needed to be embellished, whether a shawl, pillow, hand towel, or bed covering, it was pulled out and, after much deliberation, a suitable decoration was chosen.

Samplers typically depicted the alphabet and numbers. Village scenes, verses, animals, and birds were other favorite motifs. As a finishing touch, a girl's name, the date, and sometimes her town were added to the finished work.

Nowadays, antique samplers are cherished collectibles. The time-worn linen, faded yarns, and dates committed to cloth a century or more ago are quaint reminders of another age. A single sampler can set off an entire wall. Samplers also look well grouped and are often displayed side by side, one atop the other, or in various sizes with one long row.

Although many old samplers seem monochromatic, they often have brighter back sides, revealing the toll that light and time have had on these precious remnants of yesteryear. So it's essential to protect an old sampler properly. When making a new sampler (see the alphabet sampler project on page 46), give it the same loving care. That way, it will last as long as today's antique samplers.

An Alphabet Sampler

Needlecraft skills were once passed on from mother to daughter as part of the education process. Making an alphabet sampler combined learning the letterforms with practicing basic embroidery stitches. Samplers were often simple, using just one color and a few stitches, such as the one shown here. They could also be very elaborate, combining many colors and pictorial elements as well as letterforms. Each type, embracing the personality of the maker, has its own meaning and charm, and each sampler is unique.

To frame your sampler, first stretch and iron the work into an even rectangular shape. Then wrap it around either foam board or thick pH-neutral cardboard cut to a size that will fit into your frame. Clip the corners on the back side and glue down the edges. For the frame, you might use one of the handpainted techniques for frames found in the project on page 116.

You might also consider using these letters as patterns for monograms on linens, pockets, handkerchiefs, and so on. If the fabric is not suitable for counted-thread work, add a layer of cloth canvas to work over (it can be pulled out later). Or add a piece of tightly woven cotton under the monogram and cover up the edges with a border stitch.

DIRECTIONS

SIZE: Design area, approximately 10" x 12¼" (25 x 31 cm).

YOU WILL NEED: One piece even-weave fabric, 14-count (Aida cloth), 12" x 18" (30.5 x 45.7 cm); 6-strand embroidery floss, 4 skeins main color (lettering), 2 skeins contrast color; embroidery needle; masking tape.

PREPARING FABRIC: Cut a 12" × 15" (30.5 × 38.1 cm) rectangle from the fabric. To prevent fabric from unraveling, bind all raw edges by folding over lengths of 1" (25-mm) masking tape.

Each X in the figure represents one cross-stitch. Count squares in the figure and threads on the fabric to embroider cross-stitches that will correspond to the Xs in the figure. Cut the floss into lengths of about 18". To center your work, fold the fabric in half both horizontally and vertically, and mark the center with a pin. Begin at this pin mark with the stitch arrived at by following both arrows in the figure. Unless your fabric is stiff, work in an embroidery hoop.

CROSS-STITCHING: To begin, leave a little tail of floss on the back and work over it with the next few stitches to secure it. Work all underneath stitches in one direction and all top stitches in the opposite direction, making sure all strands lie smooth and flat. Occasionally, let the needle hang freely from your work to untwist the floss. Make crosses touch by inserting the needle in the same hole used for the adjacent stitch. If there are several Xs in a row on the chart, you may want to work a number of half cross-stitches, then go back to complete them all. For single stitches, it may be easier to make complete cross-stitches. To end off, insert the needle in a few stitches on the back, then clip the floss close to where it emerges.

FINISHING: Use 3 strands of floss in your needle and work each cross over 2 horizontal and 2 vertical threads of the fabric. Follow the figure cross by cross from the center out to the edges. Leave a margin of blank fabric all around. Mount and frame the sampler as you wish.

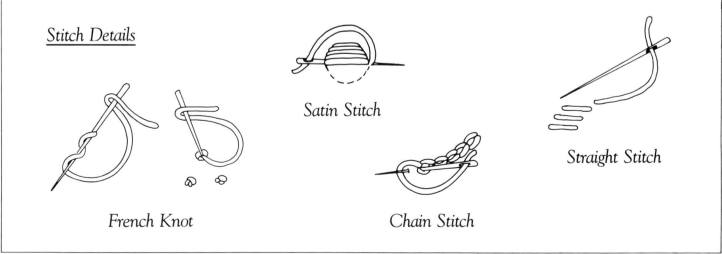

Stitch Details

Satin Stitch

Straight Stitch

French Knot

Chain Stitch

Experts in textile restoration offer the following tips for caring for an old sampler: Check to see that the sampler is not mounted on wood or regular paper; their acids can be damaging. Instead, mount the sampler on linen, which adds texture, or acid-free paper. Because old samplers are often dry, brittle, and thinner than quilts, be sure to protect them by placing them under glass. The glass keeps them from being dislodged when they are dusted.

When having the sampler framed, make sure the glass isn't touching the fabric. A professional mounter will provide a "fill," usually made of mat board, to hold the glass away from the fragile material.

It's also necessary to protect a sampler from the elements. Don't hang it in the bathroom, near an open window, or over a radiator, stove, or other source of heat. To prevent unwanted fading, keep the sampler away from bright or direct light. Similarly, if it is displayed under art lights, use the lights only when showing off the piece.

They look old, but these wee samplers (above) are all new, sent to their Florida owner, a transplanted Minnesotan, from a friend back home. A motif from the sampler (right) inspired the stenciling above it. In a Virginia stone house (opposite), an American eagle keeps watch over a symmetrical arrangement of English and American samplers bordered in old and old-style frames. Time-worn wooden boxes and chests are stacked beneath. Contemporary folk artist Bill Duffy carved the playful leopard.

Embroidered Napkins

In Colonial times, reusing or repairing worn fabrics was often a necessity. Patchwork quilts are a prime example of frugal recycling. Other inventive ways of using every available scrap of fabric can be seen in both clothing and household items. Embroidery, in the same way, was often a form of mending. Worn table or bed linens would be cut down and made into smaller items such as towels or napkins, and embroidered to cover flaws, rips, or stains.

Today, cloth napkins make pretty table accessories, and with the availability of machine-washable, no-iron fabrics, they can be practical for everyday use. The napkins shown here are charming and easy to make, especially if you have a sewing machine capable of embroidery.

This napkin was machine-embroidered on a Viking® 6690. Instructions are given for both hand and machine embroidery (with specific instructions for the Viking in parenthesis).

DIRECTIONS: MACHINE EMBROIDERY
SIZE: 18" (45.7 cm) square, including fringe.

YOU WILL NEED: White, finely woven fabric, one 18" square for each napkin; sewing thread in navy or desired color; stabilizer (or tissue paper); water erasable fabric-marking pen; ruler; scissors; iron.

CUTTING: Cut an 18" square of fabric along the grain. Pull a thread 1" (2.5 cm) from each cut edge. Cut a piece of stabilizer the same size.

STITCHING BORDER: Place the stabilizer under the napkin. Stitch the borders around, making sure to stitch through the stabilizer as follows: Using the pulled thread as a guide, sew all around the napkin with the Point de Paris stitch or any stitch similar to a blanket stitch. The stitches will pull the threads together where the fringe will start, and the legs of the stitch will lock into the woven area, preventing further raveling.

CROSS-STITCHING: Using the edge of the presser foot as a guide, stitch cross-stitches inside this border.

STITCHING CORNER MOTIF: If your machine has a programming function, program a flower (B-8) and/or a leaf (B-7). Press the Repeat button. Press the Finish button. Stitch the flower in one corner of the napkin. Press the Repeat button and Finish button and stitch another flower in the same way. Repeat the procedure to make three flowers in one corner of the napkin, stitching them so all stems meet at a point.

FINISHING: Remove the stabilizer. Pull the rest of the edge threads up to the Point de Paris stitches to make the fringe. Press the napkin.

DIRECTIONS: HAND EMBROIDERY
SIZE: 18" square, including fringe.

YOU WILL NEED: White even-weave fabric, 25 count (Zweigart cotton-rayon Lugana, available from Joan Toggitt Ltd., or linen Dublin fabric), 55" (139.7 cm) wide, 1 yard (91.4 cm), for 6 napkins; dark blue 6-strand embroidery floss; water-erasable fabric-marking pen; ruler; embroidery needle; scissors; iron.

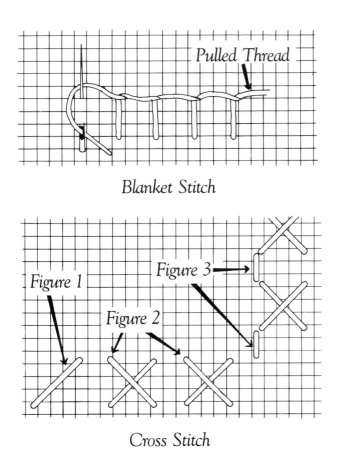

Blanket Stitch

Cross Stitch

Figure 1

Figure 2

Figure 3

Pulled Thread

Embroidery Stitches

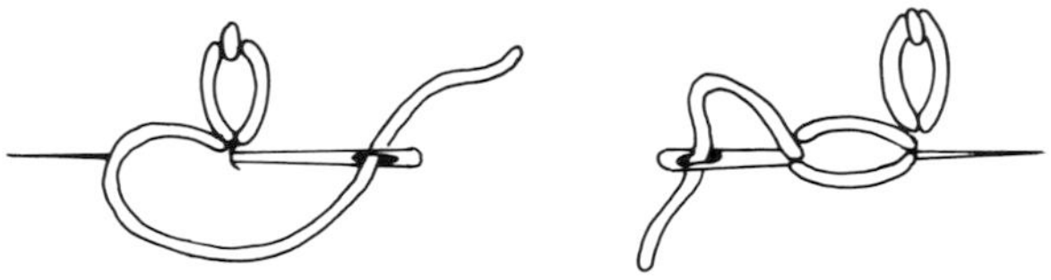

Lazy-Daisy Stitch

Outline Stitch

Corner Motif

PREPARING FABRIC: Mark 18" squares very lightly on the fabric with the marking pen. (Do not cut out the squares at this time.) Separate the floss and work with 2 strands in the needle throughout. When stitching, do not make knots, but rather leave a tail on the back of stitches and work over it to secure. To end off, insert the needle under 3 stitches on the back and clip the thread close to where it emerges.

CROSS-STITCHING: Measure in 1½" (3.8 cm) from the left side edge and 1¼" (3.2 cm) from the bottom edge, and place a pin there, between the threads. Bring the needle up at the pin. Make a diagonal stitch to the upper right over 4 horizontal and 4 vertical threads, as shown in figure 1. Skip 2 threads and make another half cross-stitch. Continue in this way until you have made 30 stitches, with 2 threads between them. Then work along the same row in the opposite direction, completing the cross-stitches (figure 2). Rotate the fabric clockwise a quarter turn. Following figure 3, count down 6 threads and over to the right 2 threads to begin another row. In this way, work

30 cross-stitches on each side of the square napkin. Then connect the corners of the cross-stitches along the inside with running stitches, backstitching to form a corner.

PREPARING BORDER: Cut out the napkin along the marked lines. Measure ⅜" (1 cm) beyond the cross-stitches and pull a thread on each side. Referring to the drawings and to the photograph, work the blanket stitches so that the top of each stitch is along the space where a thread was pulled and the legs of the stitches span 3 threads and are 3 threads apart. Work all around the napkin in this manner.

STITCHING CORNER MOTIF: Measure diagonally inward 2" (5.1 cm) from a corner; mark with a pin. Lightly draw, freehand, a spray of three flowers on stems that join together at the pin mark. Refer to the actual-size pattern for the corner motif. Referring to the stitches shown here, embroider the flowers and leaves in the lazy-daisy stitch and the stems in a small outline stitch.

FINISHING: Pull the threads up to the blanket stitches. Press the completed napkin.

Turkeywork ~ Hand-Crafted Linens

Using antique hand-stitched linens in your decorating perpetuates the past and brings a nostalgic dimension to any room. Yet, newly made things can match the quality of fine old things. Turkeywork is one such craft.

Any linens distinctively stitched with bright red, or Turkey red, thread have come to be known as turkeywork. Technically, however, turkeywork is a specific needlepoint stitch once used to imitate Oriental rugs made in Turkey. Intricate hand-woven, hand-knotted rugs were the rage back in the seventeenth century, but only a few could afford the costly imports. Naturally, knockoffs appeared; many fake Orientals were created using a looplike stitch made by knotting worsted yarn on canvas or coarse cloth, which was clipped to look like velvet. This stitch came to be known as the plush stitch, or turkeywork; it was popular for upholstery fabrics as well as carpets.

Today, turkeywork is a familiar stitch used in crewel embroidery or in combination with needlepoint stitches. It has become associated with the intricate red stitching done on crisp white linens, often made for the bed. Sewing Turkey red-embroidered pillows, napkins, and table runners was a favorite pastime of immigrant women, particularly of German extraction, many of whom settled in Texas during the 1800s. Slogans like "Good Morning" and "Good Night" were often stitched on pillow shams (to make these patterns, see the turkeywork project on page 54). Verses stressing diligence and hard work were also popular: "I slept and dreamed life was Beauty; I woke and found life was Duty."

The bright Turkey-red thread was also sought-after because it was colorfast, which was unusual in Victorian times. Sometimes the same kind of linens can be found stitched with blue thread, though they're still popularly known as turkeywork.

A kitchen wall hanging of fine single-thread embroidery proclaims "Always Clean" in German (above). The embroidered red-and-white pillow slip depicts a fireside scene. These linens were found by a Texas couple during one of their many antiques-buying trips to Ger-many. A California guest room (opposite) is cheered by a fringed Turkey-red dresser scarf and Turkey-red pillow shams decorated with Victorian wisdom. The dust ruffle and quilts on the white iron "butterfly bed" continue the red-and-white theme.

Traditional Turkeywork

Turkeywork evolved during the seventeenth century when Colonial women wanted to duplicate elaborate Turkish carpet designs using available materials. The dye made from madder, called Turkey red, was especially prized. The women used a variety of simple knot, pile, and embroidery stitches on both fine and coarse-woven fabrics to make such items as chair coverings and bed rugs. Areas of knot and pile stitches were also used to create contrast to areas of flat cross-stitch.

The patterns shown here are adaptable. A child's crib quilt or pillowcase can be worked up quickly, but the patterns can also be repeated for larger-size bed linens.

DIRECTIONS

SIZE: Design area, Good Morning, 8¼″ (21 cm) square; Good Night, 7¼″ × 10″ (18.4 × 25.4 cm). Each block, 12″ (30.5 cm) square. To make the patterns full size, take them to a copy shop and have them enlarged 200%—that is, double the size shown here.

YOU WILL NEED: Muslin fabric or a white pillowcase; red 6-strand embroidery floss, 4 skeins; pencil; tracing paper; dressmaker's tracing (carbon) paper; embroidery needle; embroidery hoop; iron.

PREPARING THE FABRIC: For a quilt, cut the muslin into 13″ (33 cm) squares. For a pillowcase, open the seams along the top and bottom edges, and work one design on the front, the other on the back.

TRANSFERRING THE DESIGN: Trace each enlarged design on tracing paper. Pin the tracing on the fabric, centering it carefully. Insert the dressmaker's carbon paper ink side down; go over design lines with a dull pencil.

STITCHING EMBROIDERY: Place the first area to be embroidered in a hoop, to keep the fabric taut. Begin

stitching by leaving an end of the floss on the back and working a few stitches over it to secure. To end a strand or begin a new one, weave the end of the floss under the stitches on the back; avoid making knots.

Use 3 strands of floss in the needle. Refer to page 47 for Stitch Details. Use the chain stitch for the stems and vines. Use the outline stitch for the letters, fairy, bird, flowers, and leaves, working the interior details with the straight stitch.

FINISHING: Press the embroidery lightly from the back, working on a well-padded surface. Assemble the blocks into a quilt. (Refer to the assembly and finishing directions for the log cabin quilt on page 88.) Stitch the top and bottom edges of the pillowcase together again.

Assorted prized linens (right, clockwise from top) include a bedcovering of quilted cotton further embellished by cross-stitched swans; embroidered pillowcases made in Pennsylvania in the 1920s, a prolific era for American embroidery; and rows of contemporary machine-stitched embroidery, which can give ordinary pillowcases a countrified air. Each type of stitchery has its own distinctive look; crewel bed hangings and bed valances (opposite) have the free, naive, open look that characterizes North American crewelwork. (European crewelwork has a denser, heavier appearance.) The Ontario woman who did the crewel was inspired by homes she saw in Historic Deerfield, Massachusetts. She fashioned her designs after decorations found on an eighteenth-century chest she owns. The pineapple quilt on the bed was started by a Canadian woman in the 1870s and finished by her granddaughter in the 1920s. Antique hooked rugs come from several Canadian provinces; the blue one from Nova Scotia imitates an Oriental rug.

A Crewel Embroidered Blanket

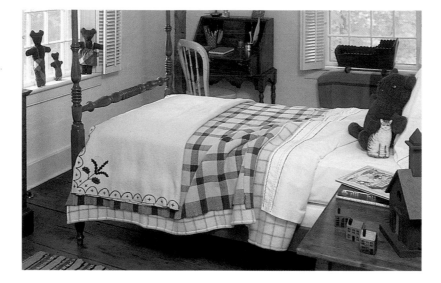

B ed linens presented a real embroidery challenge for the eighteenth-century woman. The master bed was often draped with several valances, a head cloth, side curtains, a bedspread or coverlet, and various sheets and pillow covers. All were targets for the embroiderer's needle. However, the primary function of all this yardage was warmth. Few families could afford to keep a fire going through the night. The colder the climate, the heavier the bed coverings became, sometimes actually being looped bed rugs. The curtains also provided privacy, for the master bed was often in the main keeping room. Because both family and visitors gathered here, there was considerable social pressure to make the bed linens highly decorative.

The blanket shown here is a relatively simple project, using only one color of yarn and a premade blanket, but the effect is striking. Use a yarn color that coordinates with the other colors in the room and contrasts with the blanket color for best effect.

DIRECTIONS

YOU WILL NEED: Off-white wool blanket; 3-ply Persian wool in desired contrasting color (here, navy blue); tissue paper; pencil; pins; dressmaker's marking pencil; crewel needle; embroidery hoop (optional); iron. Note: Check Persian wool for color fastness or plan to dry clean the embroidered blanket, so that the yarn color does not bleed into the blanket.

MARKING THE DESIGN: Trace the actual-size pattern on to tissue paper 4 times. Pin one tracing securely to each corner of the blanket, positioning the dash lines a scant ¼" (6 mm) from the blanket edges. Using a dressmaker's marking pencil, draw same-size scallops along each blanket edge to meet the corner designs; adjust the lengths of the scallops if necessary so they connect neatly to the corner designs.

STITCHING: If your blanket is a heavy-weight, work with a full 3-ply strand of yarn. For a light- or medium-weight blanket, separate the strands of Persian wool and work with a 2-ply strand in the needle. Use an embroidery hoop if you wish. Avoid making knots on the wrong side or the back of the blanket; rather, start by working over the end of the yarn for a few stitches. To end off, guide the needle under a few stitches, and then clip the tail end of the yarn close to the surface where it emerges. Work each corner design right through the tissue paper.

Work the leaves and flowers on the stems in the satin stitch. Work the stems in the outline stitch, stitching over the center of the flowers and leaves. Also work the scallops in the outline stitch, and interrupt each scallop at the top of its arch to work the cross-stitch centered under it.

When the stitchery is complete, gently tear away the tissue paper. Using a dry iron and working on a padded surface, lightly press the blanket from the wrong side.

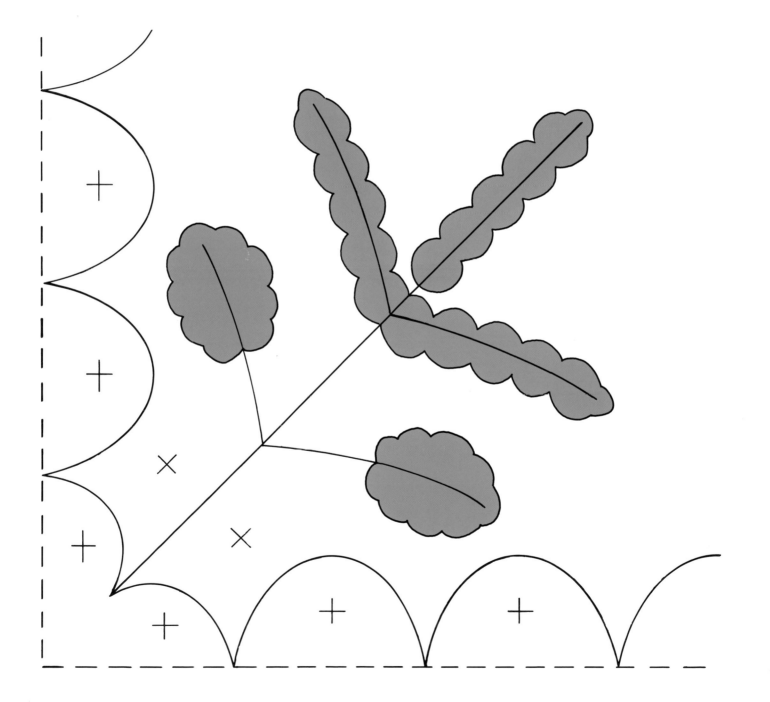

Embroidered Place Mats

The term "crewel embroidery" evolved to mean stitchery done on a ground other than canvas mesh, as in needlepoint. In crewelwork, the cloth shows through most or some of the design, providing additional color and texture. This yields a strong design that can be worked up quickly and easily.

These flower-basket place mats add yet another dimension to the design—some of the open areas of background cloth are painted. While the flower-basket theme was often used in embroidery, stenciling, and quilting projects in Colonial times, shaping the mats and adding a lacy border bring them into the modern age.

DIRECTIONS

SIZE: 11″ × 20″ (27.9 × 50.8 cm).

YOU WILL NEED: Tightly woven white linen or cotton fabric 44″ (111.8 cm) wide, ⅝ yard (57.2 cm) per mat; blue and green fabric dye or paint; DMC 6-strand embroidery floss in dark blue #824, dark green #986, dark brown #938, yellow #742, orange #946, shaded yellow-orange #51; scalloped lace trim, 1⅝ yards (148.6 cm) for each mat; white sewing thread; pencil; large sheets of tracing paper; dressmaker's tracing (carbon) paper; paintbrush; sewing and embroidery needles; sewing machine; steam iron.

PREPARING THE FABRIC: Wash fabric to preshrink it; iron it smooth. Enlarge the pattern by taking it to your local copy shop and having it enlarged 200%—that is, double the size shown here. Note: The pattern is a half-pattern. To complete it, trace on tracing paper, flip the tracing, and tape it to the first copy, matching the dashed lines. For ease in transferring the final design, retrace the complete pattern on a larger sheet of tracing paper.

TRANSFERRING THE PATTERN: Pin the complete pattern on the fabric, making sure the dashed lines line up with the grain of the fabric and the outline is ⅜″ (1 cm)

from the fabric edges. Insert the dressmaker's carbon paper, ink-side down, between the tracing and the fabric. Go over all the heavy, solid lines and dots (do not transfer dash lines or colored lines). Repeat for each place mat, spacing them ¾″ (1.9 cm) apart. Do not cut out the mats at this time.

PAINTING: Cover your tabletop with newspaper. Following the manufacturer's instructions, mix a weak solution of fabric dye and a textile medium or water. Practice brushing it on a scrap of the fabric. Strive for a light, watercolor shade of color, but not so watery that colors flow out of one area. When you have achieved this consistency, paint each place mat: Paint the leaves green and the scallops at the bottom of the basket blue. Heat-set the paint, following the manufacturer's instructions.

STITCHING THE EMBROIDERY: Use 3 strands of floss in an embroidery needle throughout. Refer to Stitch Details on page 47. Ignoring the outline of the place mat, outline

the basket and scallops, and work a diagonal lattice and vertical stems in the dark blue outline stitch. Outline the leaves and work their center veins in a dark green outline stitch. Satin-stitch the flowers as follows (short colored lines on the pattern indicate the direction of the stitches): On the center flower, work the inner ring in yellow, the outer round of petals in orange. On the flowers to either side of the center, work between the middle and outer rings in shades of yellow-orange. Using dark brown, outline-stitch around the inner and middle rings of the side flowers and make the stamens on the center flower. Also using dark brown, make a French knot for each dot on the pattern.

FINISHING: Cut out the embroidered place mat ⅜″ beyond the marked outline, leaving a seam allowance all around. Beginning at corner, pin lace trim all around the mat, with the straight edge of the lace covering the marked outline and the scallops facing inward. Be especially generous when pinning the trim around the corners, so the lace will fan out flatly around the corners of the finished mat.

Baste along the marked outline. Lay the mat on the top of the remaining fabric (for backing), with right sides facing each other. Pin to secure. Machine sew along the basting stitches; leave 6″ (15.2-cm) opening in the center of the bottom edge. Cut out the bottom layer (backing) even with the top piece, then clip into the seam allowance at the curves and across the corners. Turn the place mat right side out, turning the open edges to the inside, and press. Top-stitch close to the edge all around.

Basic Country Sewing

Sewing things is still the thriftiest way to decorate a home—and certainly one of the most creative. Home sewing has just the right look, with exactly the right detailing, in the perfect size.

Curtains, tablecloths, pillows, and blanket covers are just a few of the many projects anyone can undertake confidently with a knowledge of basic sewing skills. Bedspreads and ruffled shams require a bit more expertise, but they are still within the range of most home sewers.

Because the country look has become so popular, it's easy to find the fabrics needed to turn sewing dreams into reality. Lace by the yard, classic checks and plaids, and dainty calico florals abound in well-stocked fabric stores, crafts and quilting shops, and booths at antiques shows catering to country aficionados.

An embroidered cushion framed with ruffled chintz pillows, a tablecloth with a crocheted border, and a handmade quilt draped over the stair railing turn the upstairs hallway of a Connecticut Colonial (below left) into a cozy nook for afternoon tea. Using one pattern everywhere gives any room an instant "look." Case in point: a bedroom (below right) done head to toe in checks. Heirlooms for the future in an attic bedroom (opposite) include a quilt with trapunto stitching, handmade pillow shams, a nest of pillows in the window seat, and a double-layered window treatment that includes Austrian shades.

Short-Cut Decorating

When a large amount of yardage and great looks are called for, think of sheets. A twin flat sheet yields about 4 yards (3.6 m) of 44-inch-wide (111.8-cm-wide) fabric; each larger sheet size provides a yard more, with a king flat sheet offering about 7 yards (6.4 m) of material. Standard pillowcases equal ⅔ yard (61 cm), a king-size pillowcase about a yard. Their comparatively low price per yard also makes sheets an economical choice. Any room of the house can benefit from the color and pattern coordination of today's sheets.

Any store with a domestics department stocks sheets that capture the country spirit. Such perennial favorites as romantic floral-print sheets make wonderful gathered skirts for dressing tables or sinks. Keep an eye out for less expensive calico-print sheets. These designs can be charming when cut into napkins, table runners, or seat pads for chairs. Some sheets may have two or three coordinating prints, which can be mixed and matched to suit a particular room. If three patterns of sheets look great on a bed, try them with coordinated pillows massed in a cozy window seat. A printed flat sheet might make a wonderful ruffled valance at the window—either a bedroom window or the window in the back door.

Curtaining an old tub with lush, lined folds of bordered sheets is a dramatic gesture in a feminine bathroom/dressing room redo (above). Bedrooms decorated with sheets include an Irish bedroom (opposite above) with handmade bed hangings, dust ruffle, deep-ruffled chair cushion, and valance, each in a different blue-and-white print.

Another bedroom (opposite below) combines antique whitework bedding with a new duvet cover and matching pillows; the coordinating valances and table underskirt anchor the sunny window nook.

Knotted netting is the airy topping for a reproduction four-poster bed covered with quilts (above). The bridal-suite bed in a Connecticut inn is a frothy confection (left), with sheer, snowy curtains topped with a halo of ruffles. Straightforward blue-and-white checks create a classic country canopy in the master bedroom of a Massachusetts home (opposite left).

The same checks cover the lofty feather tick, where the family cat loves to snooze. Encircling the top of the tester bed, a ruffle of watercolor-striped fabric makes a feminine statement in the bedroom of a Finnish estate (opposite right). Coordinating fabrics finish the look.

Bed Hangings:
The Crowning Touch

Beds began as simple straw or feather pallets on the floor of the keeping room, where most country families slept by the hearth. The first bed hangings were merely fabrics strung from the ceiling beams. This created a "backstop" of sorts, to hem in warmth from the fire and from the bodies of kin sleeping side by side.

It wasn't until the 1700s that the bed, now raised up on frames, earned its own room in the house. And when the eighteenth-century householder found her bed was cold and drafty, she copied an idea from the royal and wealthy: she surrounded the bed with curtains and topped it with a canopy. Of course, this led enterprising women to seize an opportunity for creativity. They began to stitch, embroider, crewel, and crochet fabrics to make them more attrac-

tive. As homes became snugger and folks more well-to-do, bed hangings outlived their original purpose of providing warmth, and most became purely decorative.

Today, few families require bed drapes to keep them warm at night. But there is still no finer sight than a stately fourposter with matching feather tick and valance or brightly colored bed hangings (see the four-poster bed hanging project on page 68). The canopy bed remains every little girl's favorite place to dream, with the airy freshness of its hand-knotted canopy and the feminine luxury of a bed draped with white embroidered panels and topped with a snowy ruffle. And bed drapes can still be hung from the ceiling, just as our ancestors did years ago.

Four-Poster Bed Hangings

The fourposter bed radiates charm and romance, especially when it is decorated with canopies or curtains. This project shows a fresh country version of bed hangings in a crisp, pretty chintz. You might consider other fabrics on the outside and coordinated stripes or contrasting solids as curtain liners. You can also tie back the bed curtains to the bed posts using one of the tieback ideas in the project on page 74.

DIRECTIONS

SIZE: To fit a standard double bed, 54" x 75" (137.2 x 190.5 cm) with posts that are 78" (198.1 cm) high. Adjust the size and material amounts to customize bed hangings for a particular canopy bed.

YOU WILL NEED: Cotton chintz, 54" (137.2 cm) wide, 8¾ yards (8 m) each for outer panel and lining (the curtains shown are lined with the same fabric); ½ yard (45.7 cm) of coordinated solid or same fabric for tabs; sewing thread to match fabrics; pencil; yardstick; scissors; household string; pins; sewing machine; steam iron.

CUTTING: For each panel (four are shown on the canopy bed in the photograph), cut a 77" (195.6 cm) length of fabric, cutting across the entire width of the fabric. Cut the lining fabric the same size. For each panel, cut 7 tabs, each 2½" x 10" (6.4 x 25.4 cm).

MAKING TABS: With the right side of the fabric facing up, place a string lengthwise down the center of each tab. Fold each tab lengthwise in half, with the right side of the fabric inside, encasing the string. Stitch ¼" (6 mm) from the edges along one short side, backstitching over the string end to secure it, and along the long edge. Pull the free end of the string to turn the tab right side out; then remove the string. Press each tab so that the seam runs along one side edge.

ATTACHING TABS: Pin the tabs across the front of the fabric panel as follows: Place one short edge of each tab even with the short (top) edge of panel; space one tab 1" (2.5 cm) from either top corner, the rest in between, 7½" (19.1 cm) apart. Baste ½" (1.3 cm) from the top edge to secure the tabs.

ASSEMBLING: Pin each panel and lining together with the right sides facing each other and all edges even. Stitch 1" from the edges, but leave an 18" (45.7-cm) opening along the bottom of one side edge for turning. Clip into the seam allowance across the corners, then turn the curtain panel right side out. Press, turning the open edges in. Top-stitch all around the panel, ¼" from the edges. Top-stitch across the top and bottom edges again, ½" from the first line of stitching.

FINISHING: Remove the side rails from the bed canopy. Slide the tabs of the curtains on each end of the rails. Then replace the rails on the posts.

Dish Towel Valances

Take a second look at fabrics used to make tea towels, dish towels, napkins, tablecloths, and other kitchen linens. The patterns and motifs range from bright and cheerful geometrics to intricately woven variations of fruits and flowers, while the fabrics are usually fine linens or tightly woven cottons.

Often these fabrics perfectly complement a country room, so all the more reason to use them for decorative purposes. Here, for example, dish towels are folded in half to make simple but effective valances in a living room.

DIRECTIONS

SIZE: To fit most standard windows.

YOU WILL NEED: For each valance, a generously sized dish towel or one of the following: checked cotton or linen fabric imitating dish toweling (as shown in the photograph), 36"-44" (91.4-111.8 cm) wide, 1 yard (91.4 cm) per valance, or dish toweling sold by the yard, 18" (45.7 cm) wide, 2 yards (182.9 cm) per valance; sewing thread; sewing machine; iron; tape measure; standard curtain rod. Optional: small dots or squares of hook-and-loop fasteners (Velcro™).

USING A DISH TOWEL: Fold the dish towel diagonally in half over the curtain rod. You may wish to cut the dish towel into a square shape first, and hem the cut edge. If the dish towel does not cover the curtain rod, consider using an attractive pole-with-finials combination instead of a standard curtain rod.

If the valance is in the path of a breeze and otherwise needs to be secured, add a few self-adhesive hook-and-loop (Velcro) fasteners on the wrong side of the dish towel, directly under the rod.

USING YARDAGE: To determine the size of the valance, measure the distance across the curtain rod. Square this measurement, halve it, then take the square root. This number represents the size of one finished side of the

square you will need for the valance. Add 1¼" (3.2 cm) all around for hems. Cut a square this size, centering the square on the plaid or other pattern design of the fabric. Hem all around: Turn the edges ¼" (6 mm), then 1" (2.5 cm) to the wrong side, and top-stitch or slip-stitch along the first fold line. Press. Hang the valances, following the directions for the dish towel.

USING DISH TOWELING: Determine the size of the valance for your curtain rod, following the directions for yardage. Cut the dish toweling in a square the size you need. You may need to piece lengths together to achieve the desired width. To do this, place pieces alongside each other. Open out the hemmed selvages on adjacent edges and sew them neatly together, matching the pattern and determining the seam allowance so that the pattern continues neatly across the seam. Hem the cut edges, following the directions for the yardage valance.

To frame a pretty view, the side-by-side windows of this Vermont kitchen (left) are simply dressed with a swag of chintz underskirted with lace. The fabrics are draped over simple brass holdbacks at the topmost corners of the window frame, their tails trailing down to the cupboard tops. An imported embroidered valance is just the right length to cover the lower half of two attic dormer windows (opposite above). A bouquet of provincial patterns decorates the dining nook and bedroom of a city apartment (opposite below). At the window, curtains are pulled to each side with matching tiebacks by day and can be drawn at night to create an intimate atmosphere. In the bedroom beyond, a tester bed made from a kit is curtained with a coordinating fabric.

Window Dressing

Windows are the eyes of a room; they can be shaded, hidden, framed, and accented. But before they are decorated, their function should be considered. Some windows need to be covered for the privacy provided by shutters or blinds. Windows that let in too much light will need to be veiled, while smaller windows in darker rooms can often be left uncovered, with just the window frame painted for a simple but finished look.

Many country homes are more secluded, with windows facing the great outdoors. In this case, lighter or purely

decorative curtains will suffice. In fact, there seems to be a trend everywhere toward lighter window treatments these days (see the dish towel curtain project on page 69).

Tiebacks can be a great help for windows that need one kind of treatment by day, another by night (see two tiebacks projects on page 74). Country-style holdbacks of cutout tin or decorative brass can do the same job.

Swags and cornices are typical of Early American houses and are still among the most popular window treatments. Long ago, windows were smaller to conserve heat, a swag or two let in all the available light. Today, laying a length of fabric across two pegs or hooks at the top of the window frame is an easy way to swag windows. Simple swags can also be created by threading fabric through spiral-shaped metal devices, specially designed for this purpose, which are attached to the top corners of a window frame. The fabric, either lined or unlined, cascades from these knots.

Plaids and checks are favorite choices for country windows. Lace is another popular country curtain, because it admits light, affords a bit of privacy, and comes in a myriad of patterns. And good old-fashioned linen, one of America's first fabrics, offers sturdiness, texture, and an elegant well-scrubbed look.

No detail was overlooked in this blue-and-white bedroom (left and above), where windows get special attention. Lacy bow-split curtains are drawn back and accentuated by a floral wallpaper border that fully outlines each window frame and the ceiling line as well. Walls are papered in a coordinating cornflower print; fabric in the same print sheaths the curtain rods.

Tasseled and Romantic Tiebacks

Well into the twentieth century, an elaborate method for holding heavy drapes open in a formal parlor was a small but critical element in curtain design. Stationary tiebacks were carved from wood or cast in glass. Fabric tiebacks used elaborate folds and decorative bows, rosettes, and other embellishments.

The country house is also a candidate for imaginative curtain treatments. Simple or rustic tiebacks can be made with twisted or braided cords or ropes with tassels. Romantic tiebacks can include laces and ribbons, dried or silk flowers, even vines. Think about adding ceramic or glass beads, in the cording or the tassels. An imaginative tieback can be a focal point in any window treatment.

DIRECTIONS: TASSELED TIEBACK

YOU WILL NEED: Household mercerized cotton string or ecru crochet cotton #5 or J.& P. Coats Knit-Cro-Sheen®, 1 ball per tieback; 2 pencils; tape measure; cardboard; scissors; cup hook.

MAKING A TWISTED CORD: You will need 2 people to help you with this project. Have one person tie one end of the string around a pencil. Have the second person hold another pencil and stand 5 yards (4½ m) away, making the distance 3 times as long as the finished cord will be. Loop the string over the center of the second pencil, back and around to the first pencil, back to the second. Continue until you have 60 strands between the pencils, or enough to provide the desired thickness of the cord. Knot the end to the first pencil. Have each person twist their pencil, turning in opposite directions and keeping the string taut (see figure 1). When the string begins to kink, catch the center. Have your assistants bring both pencils together for one of them to hold, while you, starting from the center, slide your hand down at short intervals and let the string twist evenly (see figure 2). Continue until the cord is fully twisted.

PREPARING TASSELS: Cut a strip of cardboard to the desired length of the tassel, here 6″ (15.2 cm). Wrap the string around and around the cardboard, until you've almost obtained the desired thickness of the tassel (it will seem fuller when freed from the cardboard and fluffed out). Pass one end of the twisted cord between the cardboard and the tassel string at one end of the cardboard, until 9″ (22.9 cm) of twisted cord extends out the other side. Cut the tassel string along the opposite edge of the

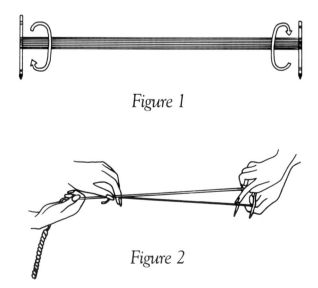

Figure 1

Figure 2

cardboard. Hold the string bundle firmly, remove the cardboard, and then wrap the string bundle tightly with another strand of string 2″ (5.1 cm) from the twisted cord. Use this string to wrap tightly around and around the tassel at this point, to form a smooth, knoblike area; then knot to secure. Fold the 9″ extension of twisted cord back on itself. Wrap the loose end to the cord with 12″ (30.5 cm) piece of string several times to secure and cover the end; knot the string to secure. Tie the twisted cord in an overhand knot close to the top of the tassel. In the same way, make and attach a second tassel at the other end of the twisted cord.

Install a cup hook in the window molding, slightly above the place where the curtain will be tied back. Catch the center of the twisted cord on the cup hook, and wrap the ends around the curtain. Tie and knot the twisted cord loosely so that the wrapped ends are hidden.

DIRECTIONS: ROMANTIC TIEBACK

YOU WILL NEED: For each tieback, ½ yard (45.7 cm) white lace-edged satin ribbon 1″ (2.5 cm) wide; ⅜ yard (34.3 cm) flat, white lace-edged trim 2¼″ (5.7 cm) wide with one scalloped edge; 1 yard (91.4 cm) double-faced pink satin ribbon ⅜″ (1 cm) wide; dried florals: 2 straw-flowers, 3 rosebuds, small sprigs of lavender, boxwood, and baby's breath; 2 cinnamon sticks; 2 silk flower leaves; white sewing thread; sewing needle; glue gun and hot-melt glue sticks; cup hook.

MAKING A COCKADE: Fold the wide lace trim crosswise in half, right sides facing. Fold the short ends together ¼″ (6 mm) twice, and stitch to make a finished seam. Open out the lace trim into a ring. Thread the needle with a double strand of sewing thread; knot the end. Make running stitches close to the straight edge of the wide lace trim. Pull the thread ends to gather the lace trim tightly; backstitch to secure the thread and fasten off.

FLORAL ARRANGING: Refer to the photograph for positioning. Hot-glue the silk and dried leaves to the center of the cockade, with the stems extending downward and the leaf tips radiating upwards and outwards to either side. Hot-glue the cinnamon sticks in a V formation. Remove all but 1″ of the stems of the rosebuds and glue the buds in a small fan shape at the center of the cockade. Remove the

stems from the strawflowers and glue them on the cockade so they conceal the glue on the other florals. Apply glue to the stem ends of pieces of lavender and baby's breath; immediately insert each stem behind the flower heads.

MAKING A MULTILOOP RIBBON BOW: Use the narrow satin ribbon. Starting 6″ (15.2 cm) from one end of the ribbon and leaving that end unworked throughout, make one 2″ (5.1 cm) loop; hold it with your thumb and forefinger. Make a second 2″ loop in the opposite direction; hold both loops in the center. Make a third loop next to the first loop. Continue, alternating sides until you have 3 loops on each side. Wrap the ribbon around the center of the loops and insert the ribbon end through the wrap, pulling it tight to knot the bow. Trim the streamer ends on an angle. Hot-glue the bow knot under the flowers, as if it were holding the bouquet together.

ASSEMBLING THE TIEBACK: Fold the ½ yard of lace-edged ribbon crosswise in half and stitch across the short ends, forming a ring. Slip the curtain through this ribbon ring, and catch the ring on a cup hook, installed on the window molding just slightly higher than where you want the curtain tied back. With the needle and thread, tack the cockade to the front of the ribbon ring, at the inside edge of the curtain.

Quilts ~ Symbols of Country Life

The quilt is one of the best-known symbols of country life. It conjures up vivid images of warmth and color, and it represents many hours of loving labor. Today, it can even be an art form, all the more cherished because time is such a precious commodity in busy lives.

New World Colonists carried on the quilting skills they'd learned in Europe, using imported fabrics or scraps of linen and wool fabric thriftily saved until America's mills began producing their own calicos in 1772. Thereafter, every general store in the country was well-stocked with a rainbow of sprightly fabrics.

At quilting bees, women gathered socially to exchange news and gossip while working on a common endeavor;

The neat classic lines and rich colors of the oak leaf quilt (above) contribute to the high country style of a Virginia living room. Hanging a vibrant quilt is an easy way to make a bold, welcoming statement in a foyer.

The symmetrical arrangement of quilt, chest, and a pair of chairs (opposite) intensifies the quilt's graphic qualities.

the quilt they produced was often given as a gift. The album quilt, popular in the mid-1800s, was also a group effort, emblazoned with verses, quotes, or pictures and signed by its makers in thread or ink. The pieced quilt is perhaps the best-known type of quilt, its design created by an intricate pattern of cloth pieces. An appliquéd quilt is covered with sewn-on designs cut from many different pieces of cloth. The crazy quilt is just that—a random assortment of pieces, usually silk, in different colors, sizes, and shapes.

Today, we are drawn to quilts primarily for their colors and designs, be they complex or simple. It is popular to hang quilts on the wall, either by the rod-and-sleeve method or by binding the quilt to a backing of muslin-covered museum board (see the union square wall quilt project on page 80).

Experts agree that quilts should be kept away from strong sunlight, whether they are hung on the wall or cover a bed. After six months of use, quilts should have six months of rest, wrapped in cotton sheets in a cool, dark, airy spot.

Quiltmaking Basics

YOU WILL NEED: Cotton fabrics 44″-45″ (111.8-114.3 cm) wide. The best results come when using tightly woven cottons, prewashed (preshrunk) and ironed smooth. Sewing and quilting thread; batting slightly larger than the size of the finished quilt (optional for log cabin quilt); pencil; transparent, graph ruler; yardstick; graph paper; cardboard; glue; dressmaker's marking pencil; scissors; sewing and quilting needles; pins; sewing machine (optional); steam iron.

MAKING THE TEMPLATES: To make sturdy patterns, draw the shape indicated in the directions on graph paper. Glue the paper to cardboard, let the glue dry, and then cut out the pattern.

ADDING SEAM ALLOWANCES: The templates show the size of the finished patch—the part that is seen when the quilt top is assembled. Seam allowances are not included in the templates or in the dimensions given for geometric shapes; they must be added for all patchwork. This frees you to use the amount of seam allowance with which you are comfortable: ¼″ (6 mm), ⅜″ (1 cm), or ½″ (1.3 cm).

CUTTING PATCHES: Lay the fabric out flat, wrong side up. Mark the patches beginning with the largest templates and proceeding to the smallest. Place each template on the fabric so that as many straight sides as possible are along the grain of the fabric. Use a sharp pencil (a light color on dark fabrics) to draw around the template. For the next patch reposition the template 2 seam-allowance widths away and draw around it. When you cut out the patch, be sure to leave a seam allowance all around. If your pattern is made of blocks, it helps to cut and store the patches for each block separately.

ASSEMBLING THE PATCHWORK: To join the patches, place two together, right sides of the fabric facing and matching raw edges aligned. Stitch along the marked lines, continuing into the seam allowances. As you work, press the seams to one side, toward the darker fabric. Patches can be hand- or machine-sewn.

ASSEMBLING: Mark the quilt top with any special quilting design. Piece fabric, if necessary, for the backing, which should be 1″ (2.5 cm) larger all around than the quilt top; cut the batting to the same size. Place the backing, wrong side up, on a flat surface, place the batting on top, and smooth them. Then baste these layers together with very large basting stitches. Center the quilt top, right side up, on top. Start at the center and baste outward in all directions.

QUILTING: Work from the center and stitch toward you, turning the quilt so that you can work outward in all directions evenly. For hand quilting, you may wish to use a frame or hoop. Use quilting thread and strive for even running stitches. For machine quilting, use sewing thread and a straight stitch, 6 to 8 stitches per inch.

BINDING: Cut the backing and batting even with the quilt top. Cut the binding strips twice the width of the desired finished binding (as noted in the particular directions), plus the seam allowance; piece the strips together so that the binding is more than long enough to go all around the quilt. Press the seam allowance to the wrong side on one long edge. Pin the other long edge to the quilt top; miter it at the corners. Stitch all around, through all the layers; trim and finish the ends neatly. Pin the pressed edge to the backing and slip-stitch it in place all around.

The Union Square Crib Quilt

A favorite nineteenth-century gift was the crib quilt, a scaled-down version of an adult quilt made for a baby or young child. Crib quilts were made in all the familiar patterns, except the patterns or blocks were on a much smaller scale. In addition to their use as bed coverings, crib quilts could be spread on the floor under a crawling baby. Young girls sometimes made tops for crib quilts, as well as full size quilts, before marriage and stored them in a hope chest.

Today crib quilts are especially prized because their size, usually about one square yard, is ideal for display on a wall. Antique crib quilts are in high demand, while new, especially handmade, crib quilts remain treasured gifts.

DIRECTIONS

SIZE: 43″ x 55″ (109.2 x 139.7 cm).

YOU WILL NEED: Fabrics—1⅝ yards (148.6 cm) for backing, 1⅝ yards for borders and patches, ¾ yard (68.6 cm) white for patches, ¼ yard (22.9 cm) each of assorted fabric for patches and binding; white sewing and quilting thread; batting; quiltmaking supplies as listed in the general instructions on page 78.

NOTE: Read the general instructions, and refer to them throughout. Remember that seam allowances must be added to all dimensions.

CUTTING BORDERS: Before preparing the patches, cut 2 borders: each 4″ x 48″ (10.2 x 121.9 cm) and 4″ x 60″ (10.2 x 152.4 cm); set these aside.

PREPARING TEMPLATES: Refer to the figures for the shapes of all patch templates. For a half square, cut out a square with sides equal to the dimension indicated; then cut the square diagonally in half and use the resulting right triangle as your pattern. Make the following templates: A, 2″ (5.1 cm) square; B, 2″ half square; C, 2⅞″ (7.3 cm) half square; D, 4″ (10.2 cm) square.

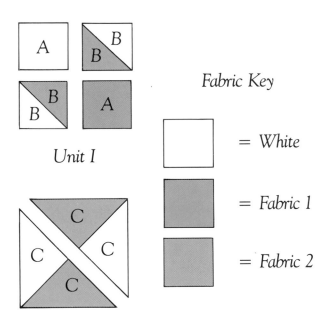

A B
B B
B B
B A

Unit I

Fabric Key

□ = White

▨ = Fabric 1

▨ = Fabric 2

C C C C

Unit II

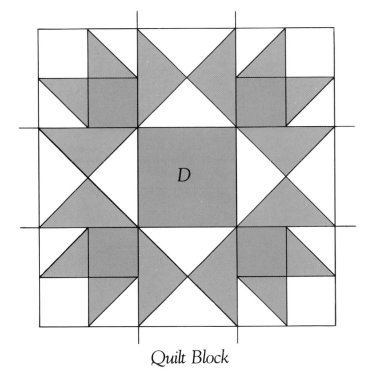

D

Quilt Block

CUTTING PATCHES: Make 12 quilt blocks, using different fabrics for fabric 1 and fabric 2 for each block. Use templates to cut out the following patches for each block: From the white fabric, cut out 4 A, 8 B, 8 C. From fabric 1, cut out 4 A, 1 D. From fabric 2, cut out 8 B, 8 C.

MAKING EACH BLOCK: Make 4 Unit Is: Stitch Bs together in unmatched pairs along their long edges to form a square. Arrange them with As as shown in the figure for Unit I.

Make 4 Unit IIs: Stitch Cs together in unmatched pairs along their short edges to form a larger triangle. Referring to the figure for Unit II, stitch 2 large triangles together along their bases; match the seams at the center.

Arrange Unit Is and IIs around a center D patch, referring to the figure for the quilt block. Stitch the units together in horizontal rows, and then stitch the rows together, taking care to match the seams. The finished quilt block should measure 12″ (30.5 cm) square (inside the seam allowances).

ASSEMBLING QUILT TOP: Arrange the finished quilt blocks into 3 rows of 4. Switch the blocks around until you are satisfied with the color juxtaposition. Sew the blocks together in each row, and then sew the rows together, taking care to match the seams. Attach the borders on each side, mitering the corners as follows: Allow an equal amount of fabric to extend at each end; do not stitch beyond the corners of the quilt top. With the quilt top wrong side up, hold adjacent ends of the border strips together at each corner. Pin, then stitch out diagonally from the quilt top corner at a 45° angle. Trim excess fabric beyond the seam allowances, and press the seams open.

ASSEMBLING THE QUILT: Mark lines across the borders, dividing them into thirds, not counting the outer seam allowances. Cut out the backing and batting and baste the layers together.

QUILTING: Stitch across the center of each block both horizontally and vertically. Stitch in the seam around each block. Stitch around the border along the marked lines.

FINISHING: Use a fabric that contrasts with the border to make a ⅜″ (1 cm) binding; attach it.

Works of Art: Amish Quilts

The Amish are known as the "plain people," yet their quilts are anything but. These brilliant graphic bedcovers express Amish skill and creativity, standing in bold contrast to their makers' quiet lives. The Amish live industriously in reverent simplicity apart from the modern world. They are farmers, with communities scattered across the United States, primarily in Pennsylvania, Ohio, Indiana, Illinois and Iowa, and in Ontario, Canada. The Amish evolved their abstract quilt patterns because their religion forbade the use of naturalistic motifs.

Though the Amish make the quilts purely for functional reasons, saving scraps of clothing and trading fabrics among themselves to get the pieces they need, the larger world has embraced Amish quilts as works of art (see Amish quilt project on page 84).

In Indiana, freshly washed Amish quilts are aired on the line (above) under the shade of an old oak tree: a garden maze with crown of thorns quilt, a wedding ring variation, and an Irish chain. A tiny Amish crib quilt is hung above a Shaker-style dresser (left). An Amish quilt from Ohio (opposite) adorns the wall of a collector's New York City apartment. Old quilt pieces have been transformed into pillows.

The Amish Bull's Eye Quilt

The Amish quilt is especially prized among quilt collectors for its striking use of color and design. Amish women often juxtaposed simple geometric shapes against dark backgrounds, but these sober guidelines did not prevent them from introducing inventive quirks and uses of color. Made from the same fabrics used for clothing, children's quilts were allowed to have brighter colors—reds, purples, greens, turquoises, and golds—while other quilts use the more sombre colors— black, gray, and mauve tones–of adult clothing.

This antique Amish quilt is pieced much like a giant log cabin block, with strips placed around a center, working outward in concentric rectangles. Perhaps the quilter of the original piece was consistent in alternating black and blue, but with time some of the colors have faded. Colors out of sequence probably indicate that the quilter used strips she had on hand, hems from dresses, or strips left over from other quilt projects.

DIRECTIONS
SIZE: 67½″ x 75″ (171.5 x 190.5 cm).

YOU WILL NEED: Fabrics—4¼ yards (3.9 m) for backing; 2¼ yards (2.1 m) for border; 1½ yards (1.4 m) each blue and black or small amounts of assorted fabrics. Additional quiltmaking materials and supplies as listed in the general instructions on page 78.

NOTE: The following directions are for the quilt shown. The size of the finished piece is easily changed by making fewer or more than the 11 rounds used here.

Read the general instructions before beginning this project, and refer to them throughout. While you do not need to make templates, you do need to add seam allowance to all pieces.

MAKING THE CENTER: Cut out a 2½″ x 10″ (6.4 x 25.4 cm) strip.

PREPARING THE ROUNDS: Cut all 4 strips in each concentric rectangle (hereafter designated a round) from the same fabric; select a fabric that contrasts with the preceding round. Make all the strips 2½″ wide. Join the strips first to the sides, then to the top and bottom edges. To determine the length of each strip, measure the edge to be joined each time.

To begin, make 2 strips the same size as the center strip. Lay the center strip vertically. Place one strip on the center strip, so that the right sides of the fabric are facing and the left side edges are lined up. Sew along the left side. Turn the strip over so that the right side of the fabric is facing up, and press. Place a second strip on the center strip, with right sides facing and right side edges even. Sew along the right side. Turn the strip right side up and press. Measure across the top and bottom edges; make two 2½″-wide strips to this length. Place a strip on the center strip, right sides of the fabric facing and top edges even. Stitch across the top edge. Turn the strip right side up and press. Place the second strip on the center strip, with the right sides facing and the bottom edges even. Stitch across the bottom edge. Turn the second strip right side up and press. Round 1 is now complete. Treating the newly enlarged rectangle as the center, continue in the same manner; and sew on 10 rounds in total.

The 11th round acts as a border. Make it 7½″ (19.1 cm) wide, and join it to the quilt top in the same way as for all the previous rounds.

ASSEMBLING AND QUILTING: Mark the quilt top for quilting: Begin at the corners of the center strip, and draw diagonal lines on a 45° angle over the entire quilt top. Mark parallel lines until you have a diagonal grid of approximately 1¾″ (4.4 cm) squares over the entire quilt top. Cut a backing and batting; assemble the quilt layers. Quilt along the marked lines.

FINISHING: Make a ½″-wide (1.3-cm) binding and attach it to the quilt.

Homage to Yesteryear

Even though popping a video into the VCR has replaced the quilting bee as a contemporary form of entertainment, making quilts—in their many colorful and intricate varieties—remains an ever-popular favorite. In fact, given its practical origins and timeless beauty, the quilt epitomizes the country look more than any other single item. An old quilt is sure to add instant heritage to a home, while a new quilt, especially one made by its user, comes with its own handstitched legacy.

Quilts were originally pieced together from scraps of fabrics or odd leftover pieces of material and lined with wool or cotton batting to be used as bed coverings. They added the only bright splash of color to a bedroom filled with rough-hewn furniture. Though traditionally used in the bedroom, where they still predominate, today's decorating makes it possible to use quilts all over the house.

Quilts come in an endless variety of patterns, including the ever-versatile log cabin design, the double Irish chain, or the wedding ring. Note that the perennial favorite of country crafts, the log cabin quilt, is detailed in the project on page 88. What continues to fascinate quiltmakers about this particular design—a central square surrounded by rectangular- or log-shaped strips—is that countless variations can be made on the basic log cabin block.

A log cabin quilt (above left) spruces up a bedroom furnished with a few carefully chosen pieces of furniture. For a quick, easy way to create a country nook in a home, just cluster a bunch of pillows on a sofa (above right). The mix of styles and designs shows just a few of the many patterns to choose from. The log cabin quilt (opposite) has been pieced together in a pattern that creates a very different look from the one shown on the facing page.

The Log Cabin Quilt

The log cabin is one of the most popular and well-known quilt patterns. A traditional log cabin block contains a center square surrounded by a repetitive pattern of light and dark strips. Folklore has it that the square represents the chimney or hearth, while the strips are the overlapping cabin logs. Patterns were often given names related to the farm, such as barn raising, straight furrows, or chimneys. The log cabin's design variations are infinite, and because it is worked in small squares that are later joined, it is portable and easy to make.

Patterns can be designed from solid or printed fabrics. Blocks can be joined directly or with contrasting borders. The only constant is the alternating light and dark pattern—two light colors and two dark colors. Contrasting colors can be placed on opposite sides of the block, or you can use a diagonal color split. Often color sequences are reversed in half the blocks, so when the quilt is stitched together an overall pattern emerges.

This quilt, shown on page 87, is a courthouse steps pattern: Strips are added to the opposite sides rather than progressing clockwise or counterclockwise. The quilt is made up of 40 pieced blocks in 8 rows of 5, which just fits a twin-size bed. You will want to adjust the number of blocks for a larger or smaller size.

Because a log cabin pattern does not have an inner layer of cotton batting, it is technically not quilted (the blocks are not sewn in a pattern to the underlayer). Instead, ours is tied to the backing fabric at intersections of the blocks.

DIRECTIONS

SIZE: Approximately 62″ x 99″ (158 x 252 cm).

YOU WILL NEED: Fabrics—6 yards (54.5 m) for backing; 4 yards (36.7 m) white for patches; small amounts of various colors for patches; 6 yards muslin for foundation; white sewing thread; white pearl cotton thread; embroidery needle; 6 yards batting for filling (optional); iron; additional quiltmaking supplies as listed in the General Instructions on page 78.

NOTE: Read over the general instructions, and refer to them throughout. Remember that seam allowances must be added to all dimensions.

MAKING TEMPLATES: To make the templates, see the figure for one quilt block, and use the following dimensions: A, 1⅛″ (2.9 cm) square; B-F, all 1⅛″ wide, in the following lengths: B, 3⅜″ (8.6 cm); C, 6¼″ (15.9 cm); D, 7⅞″ (20 cm); E, 10⅛″ (25.7 cm); F, 12⅜″ (31.4 cm).

CUTTING PATCHES: Cut 1 A patch from a colored fabric and 2 A patches from the white. Cut two each of patches B, C, D, and E from the same colored fabric and from the white. Cut two F patches from the colored fabric.

MAKING THE BLOCK: For each block, cut a 12⅞″ (32.7-cm) square from the muslin for the foundation. Sew the patches to the foundation as follows: Draw two diagonal lines corner to corner on the foundation. Place a colored A piece, right side up, in the exact center of the square, matching the corners of the patch to the lines drawn on the square. Pin it in place and stitch it to the muslin all around the edges without turning under the seam allowance. Place a white A on the colored A, with the right sides of the fabric facing and the edges lined up. Stitch along the marked seam line on one side of the white patch. Turn over the white patch so that the fabric is right side up and press. Join another white A to the opposite side of the colored A patch in the same way. Join a colored B patch to each long edge of this A-A-A row. Following the figure, continue adding patches, working outward and ending with 2 colored F patches. The finished block should be even with the foundation. Stitch it close to the edge all around the finished block.

Make 40 blocks in this way, using colors shown or as desired. This quilt uses 5 blocks each of 8 different color

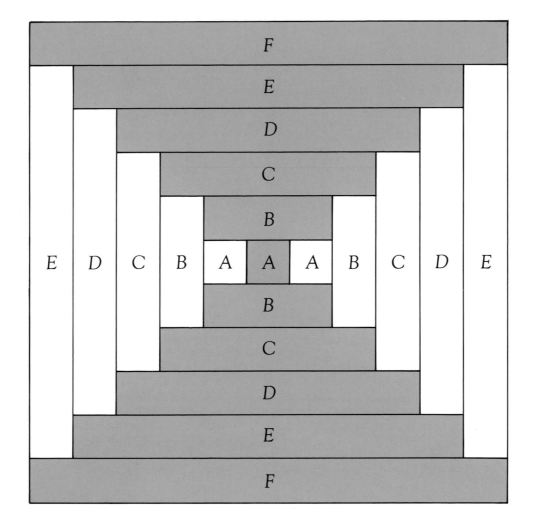

fabrics, repeating the same colors. You might want to use the same color for all the blocks, or a different color for each block, or a combination of light and dark solids and/or prints.

ASSEMBLING QUILT TOP: Arrange the blocks in 8 rows of 5. Rotate the blocks so that the colored sections are horizontal, then vertical, in alternate, checkerboard fashion; refer to the photograph as needed. Join the blocks in rows; press the seams in one direction. Join the rows, matching the seams. Press the seams downward.

ASSEMBLING QUILT: For backing, piece the fabric together so it is the same size as the patchwork quilt top. The quilt shown does not have a filler; however, you may wish to insert batting. Center the quilt top over the backing (with the batting in between). Baste the layers together.

TYING THE QUILT: Use 2 strands of pearl cotton in an embroidery needle. Starting from the back of the quilt, bring the needle to the front at the corner intersection of each block. Return the needle to the back, leaving a ⅛″ (3 mm) stitch. Cut the thread ends 2″ (5.1 cm) from the surface of the backing and tie them in a square knot. Trim the ends to 1″ (2.5 cm).

FINISHING: Use one of the colored fabrics to make a ½″ (1.3 cm) binding, and attach it.

Quilts in the Bedroom

The bedroom is the most logical place to use a quilt. Its thickness, color, and downright coziness makes a quilt the natural partner of rest and sleep. Some purists insist that quilts should be used only on beds, as they were originally intended. But this attitude tends to be the exception, not the rule.

A quilt can be the starting point for a decorating scheme; let everything else revolve around its colors and style. An inherited quilt emblazoned with butterflies or sunbonneted girls may dictate the color scheme for a nursery. The gift of a wedding ring quilt may set the tone for newlyweds' bedroom furniture. On the other hand, a quilt can sometimes be a much-needed finishing touch. A guest room's white iron daybed and white shuttered windows come alive when just the right quilts are found for the bed and for the wall.

Quilts look good next to other items that have strong graphic appeal and are often paired with Navajo rugs, checkerboard fabrics, and quilts with other patterns. An old quilt on a bed should be rotated once in a while. Any bed covering is constantly tugged at the top, which can loosen its stitching. Although switching top for bottom doesn't completely eliminate the problem, it will help prolong the life of any quilt.

The attic bedroom of a Texas farmhouse (below left) is brightened by bow-tie quilts and a basket-of-flowers pillow sham made from an old throw. A quilt takes center stage in a rustic country bedroom (below middle). Nights get chilly at this lakeside Wisconsin log house where quilts warm the bed and are shown off on a bedside ladder (below right). An old Parcheesi gameboard and graphic quilts are delightfully juxtaposed (opposite).

Quilts as Accessories

When quilts aren't quietly covering beds, they can be used for fun—as pillows, seat cushions, sofa throws, room dividers, valances, table-covers, and more. With their bright, bold look and versatile air, quilts are at home just about anywhere. Even the kitchen can benefit: Imagine a banquette cushioned with quilt-covered pillows. Throwing a quilt over a stair railing has always been an easy way to give a hallway some needed interest.

A simple sofa-and-quilt combination has great effect: Sofa cushions look lively when draped with a quilt. And the back of the sofa, usually blank when it is pulled away from the wall, is the perfect backdrop for a quilt.

Quilt lovers are always on the lookout for quilt pieces that were never made into quilts. Usually stitched to plain backings, they make wonderful pillow covers, trim for drapes, pot holders, and place mats instead.

Quilts shouldn't be hidden in a closet, but brought out in the open and used in unexpected ways. Quilts can be far more than bed covers these days.

Wicker furniture is cushioned with a collection of quilts in this Florida sunroom (above left). A schoolhouse quilt backs a contemporary sofa with a touch of country, while a child's sunbonnet quilt brightens a windowseat (above right). A few quilts were all it took to enhance a cozy room in the eaves in Oregon (opposite above). Quilts and mattress ticking are a classic combination in this sunny second-floor sitting room (opposite below).

Old-Fashioned Rag Balls

Old woolens and cottons were not thrown out in Colonial times. Rather, they were cut into strips and saved as rag balls, grouped by color and fabric type, for use in a rag rug. On their own, rag balls make charming decorative accents in a country room. Pile some made from different fabrics in a big wooden bowl and place it on a side table. Display rag balls of different colors in a small child's cradle near the hearth. Or put rag balls, some skeins of yarn, and a few antique wooden knitting needles in a big rustic basket.

DIRECTIONS

SIZE: Approximately 4″-6″ (10-15 cm) in diameter.

YOU WILL NEED: ½-1 yard (45.7-91.4 cm) woven fabric for each rag ball; scissors.

CUTTING FABRIC: The width of each strip is determined by the weight of the fabric. If you are preparing rag balls as a first step in making a braided rug, 1½″-2″ (3.8-5.1 cm) strips result in a finished ¾″-1″ (1.9-2.5 cm) braid. Cut the yardage in a continuous strip to avoid having to sew the strips together. Referring to the figure, cut along the lengthwise grain of the fabric, staying 1″ from the edge. Begin cutting again at that end, parallel to the first cutting line and 1″ from it. Stop 1″ from the opposite edge. Continue in this manner until all the fabric is cut in a continuous 1″-wide strip.

If you are cutting cotton or cotton-blend fabric, you will probably be able to begin each cut with a short snip, then hold both corners and tear the fabric almost to the edge. This will speed up the process and also give the strip rougher edges, so that the finished rag ball will have a rustic look.

WINDING THE BALL: Beginning at one end, wrap the strip around 4 fingers of 1 hand. After about a dozen wraps, slip the coils off your fingers and hold them together at the center. Then wrap the strip around the loops, placing most of the wraps in the center, with some to either side, giving the rag ball a narrow barrel shape. Continue until the center wraps are as high as the beginning loops were long. To keep wraps from slipping off the ends, start wrapping on one diagonal, then on the other. Strive for a rounded shape. After every 6 wraps or so, change the direction of the wraps, working on the horizontal, then the vertical, then on each diagonal. Maintain a nicely rounded shape. Keep working until the ball is the size (diameter) you want. If the fabric is used up before this occurs, cut another length of fabric in the same manner as before and continue wrapping with that. Tuck the tail end under a previous wrap to secure it.

Rugs ~ Art Under Foot

While hard-packed earth was flooring enough for this country's first settlers, it was only a matter of time before the decorating began. Stone floors replaced dirt and were themselves supplanted by wide wood floorboards. Floor coverings as crude as animal skins laid down for warmth were soon replaced by homemade rugs fashioned from rags or yarn.

Today Oriental rugs are reminiscent of our country's prosperous eighteenth century, when trade routes to the East opened up. In the early nineteenth century, the power loom changed the look of floors forever. The wealthy got rid of their homemade rugs in favor of machine-made creations that often imitated expensive imports from the Far East and Europe. There was also machine-made carpeting, which could cover the floor of an entire room.

Trying to identify the quintessential country rug is an impossible task. All kinds of floor coverings suit the country look. Some homeowners strive for a pure translation of the historic past, laying braided, rag, or hooked rugs on bare or painted wooden floors to mimic the earliest American homes. If authenticity isn't a first priority, creativity can come into play. Many of today's most unusual rugs are colorful renditions of subtler country cousins.

Laying small rugs on an outdoor porch (above left) shows off their colors and designs. An old hand-hooked runner from Eastern Canada spills down the stairs of a new Ontario log house (above right). Warm wood floors in the entry to a Pennsylvania farmhouse are enhanced by a pair of hooked rugs (opposite).

The Enduring Braided Rug

Braided hair, braided baskets, colorful braided rugs—lots of country favorites begin with a simple braid. While braided rugs were a typical Colonial craft, the technique is ages old. For example, the Egyptians made plaited rush mats thousands of years ago.

During the nineteenth century, braided rugs on painted floors were a common sight. The family rag bag, filled with worn-out clothing and odd pieces of cloth left over from other sewing projects, was the source of most rug materials. These discarded fabrics were cut into strips and often wound into rag balls according to color (see the rag ball project on page 94). When enough rag balls had been accumulated to be made into a rug, a new project could be initiated.

Although braided rugs can be made from new material, part of their charm is that they make use of the old. Wool makes the sturdiest braided rug, but cotton and silk fabrics are also suitable.

Underfoot, braided rugs create a rich, textural floor covering. The intertwined strips of fabric in a myriad of hues are traditionally spiraled into rounds or ovals. Heart-shaped braided rugs are always popular (see the braided rug project on page 102).

Workmanship and color distinguish a braided rug. The rug maker must envision how various colors will look when braided together and wound side by side. Surprising combinations create unusual rugs, although a subtle mix of rich, warm tones is more traditional.

The anchor for an eighteenth-century shoe-foot hutch table (far left) is an oval braided rug so large it warms the entire keeping room. The subtle tones of braided rugs set the mood in a restful bedroom (left). The vibrant braided rug in another keeping room (opposite) was woven by a contemporary Arkansas craftswoman.

Rags into Rugs

Elizabeth Eakins started her craft work based on one simple principle: She believed it was possible to produce high-quality handmade rugs. Her success has proved her right.

Eakins began making rugs quite by chance. After graduating from art school in California, she saw a friend's grandmother braiding rugs in a Vermont farmhouse and was taken with the technique. Putting her background in textile design to work, Eakins apprenticed with this woman, spending many hours working at her side. She soon began making rugs for her own house in Vermont. Friends saw the rugs and wanted ones for their own homes. One of her first clients was a New Yorker, so Eakins had a built-in client base when she moved to New York and set up shop in a downtown loft, where she lived and worked. There, she made braided rugs privately for people. Word of mouth told of her talents, and a business was born.

Eakins knew hand-weaving and was soon recycling material left over from making braided rugs to make woven rugs. Today, flat-woven rugs, designed in a wide range of floral and graphic patterns as well as adaptations of Persian styles, comprise a major part of her business. In fact, Eakins stopped making braided rugs in 1985 when the rugs proved too labor-intensive to be cost-effective. Now, a New Hampshire mill supplies the fabrics for many of her rugs. All are made of natural fibers. Wool is the primary material, but linen and silk are also used.

Although Elizabeth Eakin's rugs are modeled after eighteenth- and nineteenth-century designs and are made with only natural fibers, their cheerful colors reflect today's palette (right). Eakins' first showroom featured a number of handmade crafts in addition to her rugs (opposite).

The Heart-Shaped Braided Rug

Rugs provided necessary warmth and protection from splinters on cold wooden floors in country homes. They also provided a way to recycle used fabrics. However, few rugs from before the mid-1800s have survived, since they were used until they fell apart. We do know, though, that women made hooked, braided, and crocheted rugs on a regular basis.

A wide variety of braided rug shapes are possible: round, oval, square, rectangular, even special shapes such as hearts. Careful selection of colors produces pleasing textures or color gradations. Consider using the same color or two or three different colors for strips in a braid. Keeping two colors consistent throughout a rug, while changing the third, makes for nice, gradual color shifts and unifies the total design. Subtle blends such as tweeds or herringbones, when used in combination, can tone down stronger colors. Other design variations include shading from a dark center to a light edge and alternating the same colors in bands. This heart-shaped design is an original by Elizabeth Eakins.

DIRECTIONS

SIZE: Approximately 30″ from the inside angle to the bottom point and 60″ wide (76 x 152 cm).

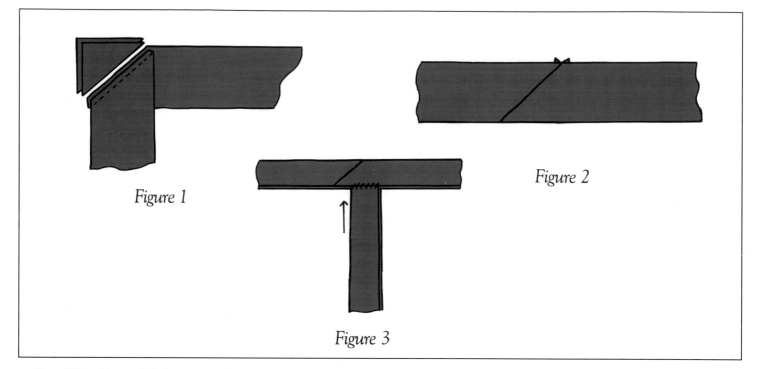

Figure 1

Figure 2

Figure 3

YOU WILL NEED: Medium-weight 100% wool fabrics in various colors (7 were used in this rug), 7 yards (6.4 m) total; sewing needle or sewing machine; darning needle or crochet hook; lacing cord such as Lox-Rite™ lacing thread; scissors or rotary cutting wheel; 3″ (76 mm) T-pins; C-clamp; elastic cord; large sheet of cardboard; small crochet hook; leather gloves or finger guards made from scrap leather; iron (optional). (For wool precut into 3″-wide rolls and lacing thread, contact The Dorr Mill Store; order a cotton kit from Distlefink Designs, Inc.)

CUTTING STRIPS: If you are cutting your own wool strips, use a rotary cutter or scissors to cut away narrow selvages of fabric, then cut other 3″-wide strips lengthwise along the fabric. Prevent tangles during braiding by rolling up each strip over a 14″ (35.6-cm) length of elastic cord, then tying the elastic ends together securely. Unroll what you need from the coil as you braid. Sew fabric strips together as necessary using a bias seam, following figures 1 and 2.

FOLDING AND PINNING: Fold each strip lengthwise in half once, then again, then again, so there are six layers of fabric that make a sort of cord about ½″ (1.3 cm) wide and thick. Secure these folds with T-pins about every 4″ (10.2 cm). Open the seams to lie flat as you come to them.

STARTING: Take 3 strips and join them in a T as follows:

Sew the ends of 2 strips, then fold them as indicated above. Insert the end of the 3rd pre-folded strip between the folded edges of the first 2 strips at the bias seam, and stitch over this securely and inconspicuously (see figure 3). Using a clamp, anchor the center of the T to a table or shelf; move the braid in progress upwards on the clamp so your work is always at a comfortable height.

BRAIDING: For regular or straight braiding, bring the right strip over the middle strip, then bring the left strip over the middle strip. Keep repeating this sequence (see figures 4-6). Keep the open edges of each strip at the sides. Hold the strips firmly and keep the tension tight and even. Use T-pins or perhaps spring-type clothespins to hold the braid together when you are not actively braiding. Make several feet of braid and then start lacing.

LACING: Thread the darning needle (lacer) with about a yard (91 cm) of cord; knot the end. Insert the lacer through a loop of braid (see figure 7) to begin lacing. Push the needle from the inside of the folded braid to the outside, leaving the knot buried.

While lacing, wear finger guards or gloves; after each stitch, pull the cord tightly, so that it is completely hidden. Keep the tension consistent. Before a length of thread ends, attach a new one with a square knot, or by following the instructions for Lox-Rite lacing thread.

For lacing straight sections of the braid, lace through a loop on the next round of the braid, then through a loop one away from your start. In this way, you will be staggering the loops; refer to figure 7. When you round a curve, which is smaller on the inside than on the outside, pick up two loops of the outside braid for each one on the inside. Ease in extra loops when the size of the rounds is increased.

SHAPING: The heart shape starts with a V-shaped braid. This V determines the size and shape of the completed rug. A cardboard guide makes it easier to start the foundation braid and maintain the shape for the first few rounds of lacing. Draw a right angle in the middle of a cardboard rectangle so that it forms a wide V shape. Beginning with the first T, make a braid 36″ (91.4 cm) long; secure the end of the braid with a T-pin. Tack the center of this braid to the point of the V on the cardboard, and baste the braid along the V for a few inches to both sides of the point. Use a thread of contrasting color so that you can easily remove these stitches and the cardboard once the shape of the heart is established. Make about 4 feet (1.2 m) more of the braid. Manipulate the braid to make a U-turn at the T-pin mark, and place it alongside the first braid.

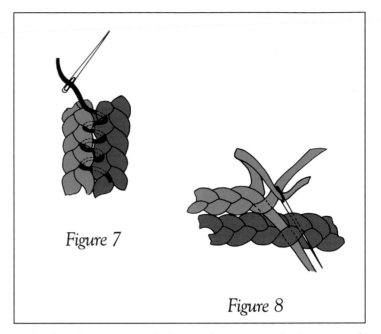

Figure 7

Figure 8

At this first turn, and also at the turn at the bottom of the heart shape, and at the turn around the center braid on the other side, add two loops on the outside braid for one on the center one. When you reach the inside angle of the heart shape, however, lace the opposite way: Add two stitches on the center braid on either side of the angle. Otherwise, proceed with straight lacing.

CHOOSING COLORS: This heart-shaped rug uses color combinations for only 1 round, as in the 2 outer rounds, or for up to 7 rounds, as in the center. For the neat uniformity of concentric hearts, change colors at about the same place in each round. In this rug, the change most often occurs along the upper-right curve of the heart.

FINISHING: When you have reached the finished size of the rug, end off at the same place where you have been changing colors. Taper the strips to a long and gradual point. Use the lacer or perhaps a crochet hook to pull each strand through a loop of the braid in the previous row (see figure 8). Take care to make this blend with the rest of the rug as neatly as possible. Pass each strand through a couple more loops for strength, then cut each as close as possible to the rug. Tuck raw ends under the last loop they were passed through.

If desired, you may steam-press the rug lightly, blocking it to a more perfect heart shape. A few bumps are normal and will flatten soon after the rug is placed on the floor and walked on.

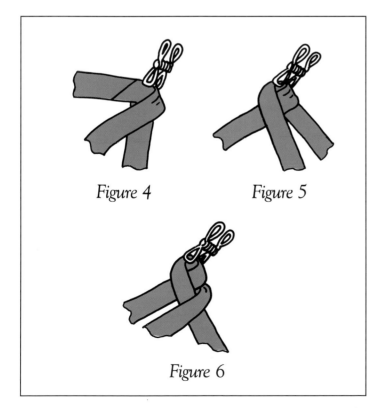

Figure 4

Figure 5

Figure 6

Down-Home Hooked Rugs

Hooked rugs have down-home appeal and lend themselves to all sorts of country settings. Often charming in their naïveté, hooked rugs can be disarmingly simple in their design. They frequently depict all variety of animals or classic scenes from nature—a basket of flowers, an apple tree. Hooked rugs with geometric patterns can be found, but those with pictorial designs seem to be most popular.

A hooked rug is fairly simple to make. First, a design is traced on a mesh backing. Then, wool yarns or scraps of fabric are punched, with a special curved metal hook, through the backing to create the rug's design.

Although many people, including scholars, think of the hooked rug as a popular Colonial floor covering, this is not true. Floors in the true Colonial house were usually bare and cleanly swept. The mention of yarn-sewn bed rugs in early inventories, wills, and literature may have contributed to this confusion. Bed rugs, or rugges, were thick, nubby bedspreads, common in Europe and Scandinavia, designed to keep one warm before central heating. In fact, it was not until the mid-1800s that floor coverings became fashionable and hooked rugs were actually made for the floor. Some of this country's earliest hooked rugs were made by thrifty householders who used available commodities; for instance, they pulled cloth rags through backings of loosely woven burlap flour sacks.

Animals are a familiar theme on hooked rugs. A contented cat welcomes visitors in an entry (above left). A new hooked rug in the center of a Lancaster, Pennsylvania, living room (above right) catches a frisky horse mid-stride. The rug is set atop mid-1900s Amish rugs. A fluffy sheep (opposite) has lived a long life on an 1840 hooked rug. A leather seat and horsehair mane distinguish the 145-year-old rocking horse.

Because hooked rugs are usually relatively small in size, they frequently decorate foyers or are positioned in front of doors or at hearthside. Several hooked rugs can be laid out on one bare wood floor; the floor acts as a frame around each one and shows off the designs. This is especially effective in a bedroom, where there isn't a lot of traffic. Another way to show off a particularly fine hooked rug is to lay it on top of another larger floor covering; a hooked rug certainly enhances wall-to-wall carpeting.

Of course, some hooked rugs from yesteryear are too precious for everyday use. This has prompted collectors to have their rugs professionally mounted, so these fine examples of a humble old craft can be displayed on the wall.

Today's hooked rugs are so authentic, it's hard to tell the old (above), from the new (opposite). These imaginative antique hooked rugs are adorned (clockwise from top), with Canadian whalers at work, a 1900s basket of flowers, and a trusty steed from the 1920s. Above a bookcase topped with folk-art fish (opposite), a hooked rug captures a playful racing scene.

Painted Effects

With Brush in Hand

There are all kinds of ways to transform a house. Paint is one of the simplest. This material can be used to create impact and effect for a comparatively small investment of time and money. Of course, paint comes in a vast array of shades, and the choices are daunting at times. But once the proper color has been picked for the desired look, just about anything is possible. Thinking of a room all in light blue or the same space painted yellow reveals the great changes a bucket of paint can perform.

Turning an ordinary paint job into something quite spectacular takes inspiration. We have only to look to this country's early craftspeople to see what they accomplished with a minimum of materials applied with imagination. Itinerant artists traveled up and down the East Coast painting projects large and small. Their legacy is a vast collection of stenciling and some priceless murals on the walls of houses both simple and grand.

In those days, one didn't have to be a traveling artist to pick up a brush and paint. Ordinary householders tried their hand at painting and decorating furniture, using common materials they found around the house. Simple woods were transformed with no one the wiser, and humble furniture took on airs. The imaginative hand, armed with a sponge, rag, feather, or comb could create elegant *faux* finishes resembling fancy woods and marbles. Stenciling was another economical method employed by nineteenth-century homeowners seeking to liven up their often drab interiors.

As testimony to their timelessness, these honored techniques all survive today. Sponged and feathered blanket chests, stenciled walls, and painted floorcloths are as popular as ever. In fact, the five paint projects included in this chapter are sure to reward anyone who decides to tackle them. All it really takes are a bucket of paint, a brush, and a vision.

The Dutch and German settlers who came to America were known for decorating their immaculate homes with cheerful colors. In a guest cottage in Texas (right), the subtly graded colors of the hallway provide a warm backdrop for a vividly painted 1850s chair originally found in Pennsylvania.

A Paintbox of Ideas

When sprucing up a plain room, hall, stairway, floor, or even the most humble, unassuming piece of furniture, handpainting is a personalized, imaginative way to give it a whole new lease on life. Primary colors make a declarative design statement, while delicate, pastel shades create a more subtle atmosphere. Painted patterns can be varied to suit any mood.

One of the easiest ways to reinvigorate old furniture or add drama to a new piece is to select a striking color that will completely change the appearance of the piece. This is as appealing in a room filled with texturally rich items as it is in a very neutral setting, because the simplicity of a single color enhances everything around it. If the furniture needs to blend with its surroundings and create a serene mood, then opt for mellow colors or perhaps echo an already-dominant color in the room. There's also the option of varying the color scheme, combining several colors in one piece. Furniture with interesting shapes and unusual curves lends itself best to mix-and-match combinations that, in effect, create a "crazy quilt" of vivid colors.

It's also possible to embellish walls, floors, furniture, or crockery with various types of stippling and handpainted designs, including marbleizing, tiger graining, and sponge painting (see projects for these techniques on pages 116 and 122). These are enjoyable crafts that don't demand high levels of expertise to achieve successful effects. For marbleizing, just paint on bold bursts of color with a paintbrush and add marble veins with a smaller one. If a mistake occurs or the color combinations don't work properly, simply glaze over them. Continue to experiment with the paint until the effect is satisfactorily created.

A quick and easy way to create rich, varied interest is by group-ing crockery stippled with several different colors of paint in an imaginative cluster (top). A chair-and-table duo take on a country botanical theme (right). Their primary colors stand out vividly against the natural wood wall. Imagine taking an old bureau or any sort of cabinet and restoring it with a highly textured marbleizing technique (above). Stippling a floor with vivid colors in random patterns (opposite) can breathe new life into any room.

Restored and Painted Frames

Painted patterns enlivened the furniture and walls of yesterday's country homes; the term "grainer" described the skilled artisan who was hired to decorate Victorian parlors. Finishes were used to duplicate precious materials as well as for their own sake. Popular *faux* finishes included marbleizing, graining, sponge painting, stippling, and pickling.

Materials used to make these fancy paint treatments included feathers, sponges, combs, special tools for wood and rubber graining and patterning, and brushes for stippling or flogging (dragging). Most are available today. (Sponged and combed finishes are featured in the project on page 122.)

Two types of finishes are detailed in this project. Marbleizing uses paint layers and fine brushes or feathers to duplicate the intricate patterns of fine marble. Graining, or simulating elaborate wood patterns, involves painting the wood with an ochre or brown undercoat and then glazing with a darker color. While wet, the surface is mottled with brushes or combed with special tools to create decorative patterns.

DIRECTIONS

YOU WILL NEED: A pleasing antique picture frame; wood glue; wood filler; artist's acrylic paints (suggested colors for the base coat include thalo crimson, thalo yellow green, and cadmium yellow; suggestions for the top coat include burnt umber, burnt sienna, and mars black); varnish stain; fine sandpaper; #0000 steel wool; tack cloth; paint scraper; disposable plastic or aluminum plates for use as palettes; small, flat paintbrushes; disposable sponge brush; paper towels; newspaper; push points (glazier points); brown paper; screw eyes and picture-hanging wire; screwdriver; any of the following tools for graining: terry cloth, clothesline, sponges, corncobs, feathers.

NOTE: It is best to practice *faux* finishes on scrap wood before applying them to a frame.

RESTORING: Reglue and nail the frame corners as needed. Lightly sand all glued areas. If veneer or plaster designs are loose or broken, soak the veneer in water to soften the glue; then reglue the pieces. Carefully pry off any areas of crumbling plaster to expose the wood underneath. Fill these defects with wood filler. Sand the frame until it is smooth.

PREPARING PAINT: Thin the paint to the consistency of cream. Pour the paint onto a palette and mix the colors.

MARBLEIZING: This is the easiest of the *faux* finishes. Suggested color combinations include black over red, burnt umber over yellow, and black over burnt umber. Apply at least 2 coats of the base color and let it dry thoroughly after each coat. Smooth between coats with steel wool. Apply a top color using crumpled paper towel or newspaper. Use only a small amount of top color, dabbing it on in a random manner. Start with the narrow inside edge and then paint the front and outer edges. The amount of paint and pressure you apply will affect the finished design, so do experiment. And if you don't like the results, simply remove the paint with a wet paper towel and begin again.

For extra drama, add veining. Dip a feather in a lighter shade of paint, and alternately draw, twist, and drag it lightly across the marbleized surface. Work generally on diagonals, but jerk and jiggle it now and then, and add finer tributary offshoots. Keep the veining soft and subtle. Refer to pictures of real marble to make these veins look as realistic as you can.

TIGER GRAINING: This technique requires a little more time and practice. Suggested color combinations include burnt sienna over yellow, black over burnt sienna, burnt umber over green, and black over red. Apply base coats,

smoothing the surface with steel wool as described for marbleizing. Apply top color with a 4″ (10.2-cm) piece of woven clothesline or a folded strip of newspaper. Lightly dip the end of your tool in the paint; remove any excess by dabbing on a paper towel—too much paint will form globs or smear. To make vertical tiger stripes, press evenly on the tool to make each stripe. Repeat across the front side of the frame. Don't worry if the stripes do not look alike. If the paint smears or looks too heavy, remove it with a damp paper towel. When the front has dried, decorate the inner and outer edges in the same manner, matching the stripes to the front.

An angled tiger stripe variation can be created as follows: Measure and mark the middle point of each side of the frame. Start at the midpoint of one side, working with clothesline or newspaper, and make a center stripe perpendicular to the edge. Working toward one corner, make the stripes with decreasing angles. When you reach the corner, the stripes should be 45° diagonals. In the same way, work toward the other corner. Work the 3 other sides of the frame in the same manner. Apply perpendicular stripes at the inner and outer edges, matching them to the front stripes.

CREATING MISCELLANEOUS FINISHES: Try different tools and textures for various effects. Rolling a corncob in a motion like the hands of a clock can produce a wonderful fan pattern. Use fingertips or thumbprints, the whole length of a finger, even several fingers together as paint tools. Small squares of terrycloth give an interesting texture as well.

For a crisp effect, paint the inner edge a dark color and sponge or marbleize the outer edge. For another decorative effect, raised corner blocks can be cut from a thin piece of balsa or other soft wood, painted a contrasting color, and glued over the corners.

FINISHING: When the paint has thoroughly dried, smooth the surface with steel wool and then wipe with a tack cloth. Using a sponge brush, apply a thin coat of varnish stain to age and darken the paint color. Paint the back of the frame with a flat black paint to give it a finished look. Place the glass and the item being framed in the frame and add a cardboard back. Secure all layers with glazier's push points. Cut a rectangle of brown paper about ½″ (1.3 cm) larger than the frame opening all around. Place a thin line of glue around the edge of the frame opening; press the paper over the back. Add screw eyes to the back and thread picture-hanging wire through them, wrapping the wire ends toward the center to secure.

Painting on Furniture

A treasured round table, hand-painted years ago with luscious fruit, is the focal point of a Florida cottage (left and above). In an attic bedroom in Texas (right), unfinished pine walls set off a tall child-size bed dated 1806 and topped with a turkey-work pillow sham. The bed was probably brought from Germany by the farmers who settled the area in the mid-1800s.

Like all homesick travelers in unfamiliar territory, American Colonists were torn between excitement about their new land and a love for the old ways. Beside their meager belongings, these settlers brought along ideas about home. In setting up their new residences, they copied the furniture designs and decorations most familiar to them.

Tables, chairs, beds, cupboards, and stools were crafted, some hastily, some painstakingly, as needs arose. If the wood was attractive, it was simply rubbed with linseed oil, but common pine, poplar, or hickory pieces were usually painted.

After the revolutionary war, grain painting and *faux* finishing became a popular pastime. Humble painted pieces were transformed into imitations of the fine wood furniture found in the grander homes of Europe. (See the project on sponge-and-comb finishes for furniture on page 122.) Ornamental painting on furniture was also popular; stenciled and freehand designs were applied to almost any free surface.

Solid washes of blue, green, and red were popular furniture colors. The paint featured ingredients like buttermilk and oxblood; the Indians showed settlers how to make paint with a base of walnut oil. Paint recipes found

in Colonial Williamsburg mention such ingredients as copperas, fish oil, lampblack, Spanish brown, verdigris, and indigo.

A trunk was the only piece of furniture most families brought to America. Packed with all their belongings, it was cast into a ship's hold, its only identification the owner's name and destination. Trunks were also among the many pieces of furniture painted both to protect the wood and to brighten the home. Geometric patterns and representational motifs such as flowers and birds were popular. Today, these antique trunks command high prices. And if found slightly the worse for wear, trunks make for challenging but rewarding restoration projects.

Once the journey to this country was over, a cherished trunk claimed a special place in the home. Often, it served as an artist's canvas, as evidenced by this finely detailed trunk embellished with scenes from nature (above). Six-pointed stars and a stylized tree of life adorn a trunk found in a Russian immigrant's home in Canada's British Columbia (opposite below). In the 1800s, Ontario was called Canada West, hence the labeling on this 1840s German immigrant's trunk (opposite above).

Paint Finishes for Furniture

Sponge painting evolved before the wide availability of wallpaper as a simple but subtly effective way to add color to the walls of a room, and it makes an equally wonderful furniture finish. The technique is very simple; one or more thinned colors are sponged over a base coat. Pickling is another paint technique in which a thinned top coat is quickly wiped off with rags, leaving a subtle color wash.

Graining and combing techniques originally required ochre and brown paints and special tools to duplicate the elaborate patterns in fine woods, but they quickly became used to create fanciful patterns that never existed in nature. Metal, rubber, and wood are typical graining tools.

Begin sponge painting by working on a small, simple chest or box and progress to more elaborate pieces of furniture. Both old and new pieces are good candidates for painted finishes. Once you feel comfortable with the technique, you might try sponge painting walls (for three wall applications, see pages 128-129).

DIRECTIONS

YOU WILL NEED: Paint for base coat, either latex or oil-based semigloss in desired color; latex, acrylic, or oil (artists') paint in contrasting top color(s); latex primer for unfinished wood; medium and fine sandpaper; #0000 steel wool; tack cloth; disposable plastic or aluminum plates to use as palettes; flat bristle and foam paintbrushes; rubber-bladed combing tool and wood-graining tool (available at art supply stores); household (cellulose) sponges or natural sea sponge (available at art supply stores and cosmetics counters); satin-finish varnish or polyurethane.

PRACTICING FINISHES: Practice either of the finishes described below first on a scrap of plywood or tagboard. Wait until you are comfortable with the technique before you work on furniture.

APPLYING THE BASE COAT: Sand furniture, using medium and then fine sandpaper. Dust it with a tack cloth. For unfinished wood, use a flat bristle paintbrush to apply latex primer; let it dry. Then work the base coat and subsequent colors in either oil-based or latex paint. Do not mix paint types in the same piece of furniture. Apply 1 or 2 coats of base paint as necessary. Let each coat dry thoroughly and use steel wool between coats so that the surface stays smooth.

SPONGE PAINTING: If you are using a cellulose sponge, cut it into irregularly shaped pieces; use a sea sponge as is.

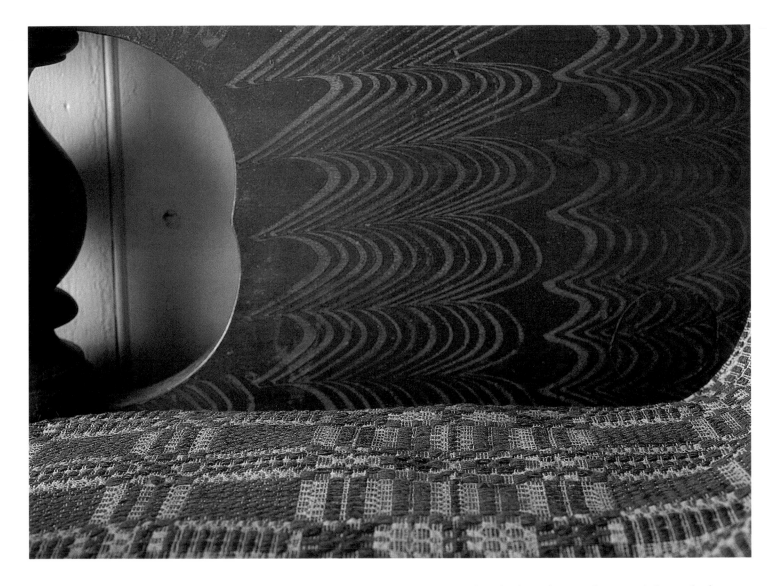

Dampen the sponge to soften it, and then wring it until it is almost dry. Pour the paint on to a palette and mix the color(s) you want. Try putting 2 or 3 colors on the palette without blending them thoroughly; the mottling that results will create a 1-step technique. Dab the sponge into the paint, then on newspaper to remove the excess. Dab the paint on the furniture, using light pressure; do not stroke on the wood. Unless you want a repeat motif, turn the sponge slightly for subsequent dabs and overlap them only slightly. Take care not to overwork any one area. If paint globs or smears, remove it with a wet paper towel and rework the area.

COMBING: Thin the paint a little (with water or paint thinner for oil) for the top coat. Work a small area at a time. With a flat paintbrush, apply the paint over the base coat. Immediately drag the combing tool through the top coat. Try these patterns: horizontal or vertical striations, fans, stripes, squiggles, zigzags, scallops, horizontal and vertical movements for cross-hatching, curves, and coils. If you are unhappy with the effect, brush over the top color and recomb. Let it dry thoroughly.

VARYING APPLICATIONS: Use sponging and combing separately, together, or in combination with flat painting. For example, consider sponge painting just the drawers and inside panels of bureau doors or marbleizing a tabletop or seat back while combing the table or chair legs. Accent the architectural details and design lines of furniture with a solid top color, or use another color altogether.

FINISHING: Seal your piece with 2 coats of varnish or polyurethane; let dry after each coat.

Dummy Boards ~ Conversation Pieces

Dummy boards are like stand-up comedians. They fill barren space, provide a companionable presence, and act as intriguing conversation pieces. These pasteboard or wooden figures have their roots in the nineteenth century, when a fireboard (often painted or stained) was needed to stop drafts from whisking down the chimney when a fire wasn't lit.

Today, snug dampers and sophisticated heating systems have made fireboards obsolete, but they are still favored for their whimsy. The height of light-hearted deceit is to place a dummy board in front of an antique mantel where no chimney exists.

Dummy boards on these two pages (clockwise from above) include a silent lady of the house with Puss 'n' Boots underfoot, a hearthside basket of hydrangeas and a pair of obedient pets, a pastel urn and fire surround painted to match a pastel room,
and for those in favor of youngsters who are "seen and not heard," an old-fashioned miss with model deportment.

Walls: Personalized with Paint

Baseboards were commonly painted black in Colonial days. But to think of Early America as shrouded in subdued and dusty tones is a bit of a misconception. Old paint chips have proven that some of our ancestors were as flamboyant with color as modern artists can be.

Walls made of logs or wooden boards were often covered with plaster—a homemade potion of crushed oyster shells, sand, and water, with a binder of animal hair. Sometimes the plaster was whitewashed with quicklime and water. However, this all-purpose cover-up had to brighten rooms that typically featured sooty fireplaces and small windows.

It wasn't long before Colonists were devising other ways to decorate their plain white or wooden walls. They made color washes out of plaster and vegetable dyes; sometimes a dose of buttermilk was added. But these concoctions had no staying power. Oil-based paints gave improved results; the earliest ones were made of linseed oil or black-walnut oil mixed with earthy pigments, plants, and minerals. Then the paints were applied with feathers, rags, sticks, combs, corks, brushes—and a bit of flair. The results were highly original and decorative.

Rubbing plain buttermilk over colored oil-painted walls and sealing with varnish was another quick but crude decoration. Sometimes plaster was grooved with a sharp instrument to imitate vertical boards. Far more sophisticated paint techniques were graining, combing, and marbelizing that gave plain walls the look of expensive paneling. A light or dark top coat painted on a wall, when tapped with a brush or rag, created a stippled or mottled look while revealing the color underneath.

As for woodwork, it was largely unfinished until the mid-1700s. After that, doors and woodwork were painted, usually in colors that contrasted with the walls.

In a restored Pennsylvania millhouse (above), old and new paints were matched as exactly as possible. It seems the miller was a pack rat who stored away an unused attic door years ago. Recently, the new owners of the house found the door, its original paint still intact. All the hallway trim was matched to the color of the door as exactly as possible. Tab curtains stitched from old flour sacks found on site pick up the same azure tones.

Inspired by a trip to Italy, the owner of a Pennsylvania farmhouse (right) painted frescoes of garlands and mythical animals in the mudroom, playfully dubbed "the Pompeian room." An ironstone pitcher collection lines the shelves. Sheetrock treated with a faux bois finish (below left) and framed with molding creates a special niche for a graceful tin sconce. The elaborate wall motif in a Prussian blue and butter-yellow bedroom (below middle) combines stenciling and freehand techniques. Free-form brush strokes and textured areas highlight a bedroom door (below right).

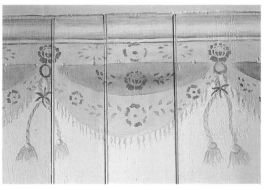

To visually enlarge the small master bedroom of this nineteenth-century Ohio farmhouse (above), a bit of imaginative painting was in order. First, the walls were rag-painted in soft, low-contrast tones, making them seem to float away. Then the floor was boldly striped to make the room seem longer. Finishing the striped boards with a solid border gives the appearance of a cheerful rug where none exists. An old farm sign inspired the color scheme for the dining room of the same house (left). Walls were sponge-painted in three high-contrast hues over a neutral bayberry base coat. Artfully sponge-painted cabinets and drawers (opposite) with contrasting borders highlight a city apartment's storage solution and are handsome besides. The top-to-bottom use of space was Shaker-inspired.

Stenciled Frieze Motifs

What is a frieze? It's the part of the wall directly below the ceiling line that's ripe for decoration in any room of the house. Just as a pretty frame enhances a picture, a frieze enhances walls, outlining the architectural structure of a room and circling it with color and design.

Stenciling's airy effect makes it especially appropriate for friezes, which seem to float in the air. A light, lacy stencil generally produces the best results, though dramatic effects can sometimes be obtained with heavy, intricate motifs.

Some precut stencils are designed especially for this part of the wall. Motifs like swags, tassels, leaves, vines, berries, and clouds—anything that hangs high in real life—are perfect for decorating a frieze. Combining two or more stencil patterns can also create a look that's one of a kind. Making original stencils or painting a frieze freehand are other possibilities. Just follow a room's natural ceiling lines, accentuating the charming eccentricities that are often present, especially in older homes.

The same type of stenciling can also work on other parts of a wall. Trimming a baseboard will coordinate the look in a room. Friezes can also border a window, accent a mirror, or decorate a wall with trailing vines.

New Hampshire stenciler Leah Caswell uses her house as a testing ground for her different stencil patterns. Between two windows (opposite), a fluid blueberry border accentuates the lines of a Chippendale mirror. The lowboy is topped with salesmen's samples. An airy leaf-and-branch motif marries well with beams and baskets (above). In her office, a tulip and swag border runs around an antique horse weather vane (right).

Her Passion for Paint

It's been almost twenty years since Sue Connell left her job as an elementary school art teacher and turned her paintbrush to antique furniture. At that time, she and her former husband were interested in starting their own business. They parlayed their backgrounds as trained painters and their love for old things into a thriving full-time business: restoring antique paint finishes on old pieces of painted furniture and accessories. Soon they were also painting interiors with the same painstaking care and authentic detailing as in days gone by.

Though Connell's work is more or less in keeping with traditional styles, she also does marbelizing, *faux* graining, and overlay painting, where layers of paint are laid down one on top of the other to create depth and richness. Stenciling is a vastly untapped area, Connell believes, though it has become "bastardized" by the proliferation of "pineapple grenades and willow trees." Says Connell, "There is a wonderful range of stenciling that is simply not

being depicted today. Some of the most beautiful stenciling was done as wallpaper." And stenciling wasn't just done on light or white walls, but on colored walls as well. "I've seen a wonderful tiny black motif done on acid yellow walls in an old historic home. Mulberry walls are nice, too," she adds. However, she cautions that stencils should be properly sized to suit the space.

Connell enjoys the serendipity of her work. She can shift from the discipline of restoring antique painted furniture to the freedom of painting murals (see page 160), depending on what comes her way. "I may marbelize for six months straight, and then do none at all for a while," she notes. A recent project found Connell painting the upstairs of an old farmhouse in the colors of nineteenth-century New Hampshire chests. Inspiration comes from everywhere—museums, books, articles, a piece of fabric, an old plate.

Connell's "folly" is her home, the 1823 Greek Revival Clayton Store. She and her 11 cats live above the store, which is "closed seven days a week." Indeed, the Clayton Store is a fully outfitted Victorian country store, complete with hats, shoes, buttons, ribbons, and more, all arranged on the original counters and shelves, purely for their owner's enjoyment.

Sue Connell's work follows a traditional style but ranges from painted murals to faux finishes for furniture to stencils. Here she has used a broad rust-colored leaf pattern border (opposite) complemented with a vertical diamond stencil to frame a grain-painted Shaker chest, painted box, Shaker finger-lap oval box, and Parcheesi board.

Walls Stenciled with History

Looking for an authentic way to decorate walls? Try stenciling. That's what the thrifty housewife did in the early years of this country, when the price of wallpaper and wood paneling forced her to look for other means of decorating. Stenciling gave the impression of wallpaper without the expense or fuss.

Today's stenciling is usually softer and more stippled than the bold patterns of the eighteenth century, when whole walls were covered in widely spaced, stylized designs combining motifs from several stencils (see the project for three traditional wall designs on page 140). Often, a continuous scrolled or geometric border was used to tie the whole thing together. (For a contemporary border, see the cows project on page 154.)

Soft-toned garlands and borders outline the bedroom window of a Texas guest cottage (above left). The owner, an antiques dealer who uses the cottage as her shop, decorated the walls of each room as they might have been in 1886, when a cotton farmer and his family lived here. Using her own hand-cut stencils and an almost-dry brush, she applied flat, water-based paints in traditional colors. The new lace curtain looks suitably aged. Adding a bit of black or brown to your paint (above right) is an effective way to "age" its color. In a guest bedroom (opposite), repeating stencils recreates the look of Early American wallpaper.

Stenciling Basics

YOU WILL NEED: Sheets of acetate; permanent black fine-point felt-tip marker; scissors; craft knife #1 or artist's matte knife; japan or acrylic paints; plastic-coated paper plates, margarine tubs, or shallow pans to use as paint trays, 1 for each color; spray adhesive; stencil brushes, cellulose or natural sponges, or velour fabric to use as applicator. Optional: hair dryer.

CHOOSING A METHOD: You can choose traditional or contemporary stenciling techniques. Traditional materials (quick-drying japan paints) and tools (velour fabric) yield a more authentic, finer texture and softer, subtler results, while acrylic paints and stencil brushes provide an easier, more contemporary approach. Water-based acrylics may be washed off if mistakes are noticed immediately.

CUTTING STENCILS: Using a felt-tip pen, trace the stencil design on acetate. Use the actual-size patterns shown in the projects, or design your own motifs. Make a separate tracing of the complete pattern for each color to be used. If you are repeating a motif over a large area, making multiples of the stencils will speed up the project. Trim the acetate sheets with scissors, leaving at least a 1″ (2.5-cm) margin all around each design.

Working on a well-protected surface, cut out those shapes to be stenciled in the first color. Use a craft knife, and make sure the blade you are using is fresh; replace the blade if it tears rather than cuts cleanly. Always cut toward you, rotating the acetate as necessary to cut curved lines.

On a second tracing, cut out the shapes that are to be stenciled in the second color. Repeat for each color.

STENCILING: Practice stenciling on tagboard or a scrap of canvas before you stencil on your wall or floorcloth.

Spray the back of the acetate with adhesive. Let it dry for a few minutes until the adhesive is tacky to the touch, giving you a temporary bond.

Press each stencil in place. You may need to add pieces of masking tape to secure the stencil, but the adhesive should be strong enough to hold the stencil in place. Press the edges of each cutout tightly to the surface.

Pour, squeeze, or dab paint on your palette. Mix colors, if necessary, until you are satisfied with the shade. (Be sure to add some water to thick or pasty acrylic paints.) Apply the paint with a stencil brush not much larger than the area you are stenciling; you can also use the other applicators listed above. Dip the applicator in paint, and pounce off any excess on newspaper, so the applicator you are working with is nearly dry. Dab lightly onto the cutout areas of the stencil; begin at the edges and work inward. Use an up-and-down motion, rather than a broad sweep. Let the paint dry slightly (a hair dryer will speed this process). Lift the stencils carefully. For repeat motifs, reposition the stencil as indicated in the directions. To reverse a stencil motif, remove the adhesive from the right side with turpentine, then apply some to the other side.

Stenciling gives this maple-leaf design (left) a properly wind-tossed look. The motif was copied years ago from an old book of traditional New England stencils, and today it graces the walls of the Texas guest cottage also shown on page 134. The soft tones and lyrical lines create a carefree effect that is difficult to capture with wallpaper. The walls in the upstairs hallway of an Ontario house (opposite) were embellished using japan paints and sponge-tipped brushes, which create soft-edged designs.

Traditional Wall Stencils

Eighteenth- and nineteenth-century homes had much more color than we might imagine. In place of patterned fabrics, paint and stencils were used on both walls and floors to create decorative effects. Combined with embroidery and quilting, this technique added color and warmth to each room.

This section presents stencils using both traditional and contemporary techniques. As you become skilled at stencils, you might want to create your own designs to suit special projects.

DIRECTIONS

SIZE: Medallion and flower pot, about 6″ (15 cm) high; vine motif, 4½″ (11.4 cm) long.

YOU WILL NEED: For traditional stencils, japan paints in dark green and brick red; denatured alcohol; scraps of cotton velour fabric; additional stenciling supplies listed in the general instructions on page 136.

PREPARING TO STENCIL: Select either the traditional or the contemporary technique, and choose stencil patterns (any or all of those shown in the right panel in the photograph, other commercially available patterns, or ones you design yourself) to suit the architectural elements of the room. Remember to practice your stencils on paper or tagboard first.

Make sure all wall surfaces are clean and dry. It is easiest to work on walls that have recently had any cracks repaired and that have been given a coat or two of semigloss paint in a light color. Save some of the wall paint for touchups.

Trace actual-size patterns onto acetate. Use the registration marks or a fine line with a cross at either end: These marks will help you align the next stencil for the second color.

The medallion and flower pot motifs are shown as half patterns (as indicated by the long dashed lines). To complete a half pattern, trace twice on tracing paper, flip one

tracing, and tape it to the other one, matching the dashed lines. Then retrace the complete pattern on one large sheet of tracing paper, and transfer the pattern without the dashed lines on to acetate. Cut a stencil, referring to the general instructions, for each color used in the motif.

MARKING: Plan your motif arrangement carefully. Using chalk or light pencil lines and a yardstick, mark guidelines to ensure that you are working on a level horizontal that is parallel to the floor and ceiling and a vertical that is either plumb or in keeping with the vertical moldings or corners. Space repeat motifs to take best advantage of the whole area available.

STENCILING: To stencil using the traditional method, cut velour into 4″ (10.2 cm) squares. Wrap one around your finger. Pour alcohol and japan paint into separate containers. Dip your velour-covered finger first into the alcohol, then into the paint. Use an up-and-down dabbing movement; do not swirl or stroke on the paint. Begin at the edges of the cutout and work toward the center. This ensures beautifully dimensional shading.

APPLYING THE MEDALLION: First position the stencil with the five circles (red in the photograph), aligning the registration marks on the vertical. Stencil the circles. Let the paint dry before removing the stencil. Use the traced but uncut lines of the circles on the second stencil to align the stencil for the second color (dark green here). Stencil, let the paint dry, then remove the stencil.

STENCILING THE FLOWER POT: Position the stencil with the leaves, stems, and pot cut out (green in the photograph), aligning the registration marks horizontally. Stencil these areas; let them dry. Use the traced but uncut lines on the second stencil to align the stencil for the second color (red here). Stencil, let the paint dry, then remove the stencil.

ADDING THE VINE: The pattern is a one-color motif that can be repeated for a long border design. To speed up the process, trace the motif 2 or more times on to long rectangles of acetate, matching up the registration marks. Make several identical stencils. Plan your spacing carefully if you intend for this motif to turn a corner. Stencil, let the paint dry, then remove the stencil.

Vine

Medallion   Flower Pot

A Painted Cottage in Texas

This guest house in Columbus, Texas, is a time capsule of sorts: Itinerant German artisans stenciled the walls more than 100 years ago. In 1968, its present owner spotted traces of the pattern-box stenciling beneath soot and dust on the walls of the cottage in her hometown of Alleyton, Texas, 70 miles west of Houston. She decided then that she wanted to own the cottage, and ten years later, the owners since 1916 sold it to her. She moved it three miles to Columbus. Today, fully restored to its former beauty, the cottage offers bed-and-breakfast accommodations.

Lacelike motifs decorate the walls of the two bedrooms in the Texas cottage (above and opposite) and work well with cross-stitched muslin curtains (left). The bedrooms flank a center hallway, the only area with a stenciled ceiling (above right). Deep color on the lower portion of the walls creates the effect of wainscoting (below right).

Checkerboards can be as interesting in muted, similar colors (above) as they are in the familiar black-and-white. Painted floors echo autumn tones in a dining room (far left). A maple leaf from the yard of this Wisconsin inn (left center) provided the image for the entry floor and stairs. An Ohio house has a stenciled staircase and checkerboard rug (left).

The Decorative Painted Floor

The colorful old kitchen of this Massachusetts bungalow (above) bursts with cheer, with the classic black-and-white painted checkerboard floor setting the stage underfoot. Bright yellow Hitchcock chairs circle a table set with pieces from the owner's collection of colorful dishware. Today, *bright blue plates, a pitcher, and a teapot are paired with pretty pink bowls. A weathered, seatless child's chair and a blue bowl filled with pears are poised atop a cupboard, welcoming all who enter through the bright blue door.*

Nothing makes a room come alive like a painted floor. Rugs have their place, and carpets are cozy, but painted floors are fun.

The painted floor is an American tradition, although the fastidious housewife of the late 1700s was thinking only of practicality. When she found her soft pine plank floors splintering underfoot, she usually applied several coats of paint to cover the entire floor or at least the border surrounding a rug. Not only did the paint hide the floor's condition, it made it easier to clean. Paint colors ranged from somber black, gray, and dark green to livelier brick red, mustard, and pumpkin.

Stenciled floors improved on the concept. They were often painted in the best rooms and the bedrooms of the house. Stenciling stars or flowers randomly across a floor was one option. Dutch settlers in New York's Hudson River Valley stenciled their floors with small geometric designs that often resembled the decorated tiles of their homeland and reflected the Dutch love for ornamentation.

Equally popular, after about 1840, was the decorative and practical spatter-painted floor. Once a floor's base coat of paint had dried, other drops of colors were splattered on top of it, either by tapping the wet paintbrush with a stick or by flicking it around.

Painted floors are once again in vogue, and the techniques used 200 years ago are just as applicable today. Spatter-painted floors and stenciling are appropriate in any setting. The classic checkerboard is far and away the most popular design. It is as suitable for foyers as it is for kitchens and dining rooms. Painted floors have punch that plain wood can't match.

Paints left over from redoing all the other rooms in this turn-of-the-century Pennsylvania house were used to splatter a kitchen floor with vivid color (opposite). Regular wall paint was used for these stenciled kitchen "rugs" (clockwise from top left). Their varnish coating wears faster than polyurethane, yielding a desired old-time look. A scattering of stencils dots a nursery floor. An old staircase in a Bucks County, Pennsylvania, canal house was treated to a variety of hand-painted motifs. Bear-paw stencils evoke the look of an appliqué quilt on the old wooden floors of an 1840s farmhouse.

Floorcloths ~ "Colonial Linoleum"

For a practical floor covering that's also decorative, consider the floorcloth. It can anchor a seating area, distinguish a dining room, cheer a bedroom, or spark up an ordinary entry.

Modern-day aficionados have dubbed the floorcloth "Colonial linoleum" because of its prevalence in eighteenth-century kitchens. The first cloths were laid over bare-wood kitchen floors where rugs or carpets were impractical. Like linoleum, the floorcloth has proven its practicality. Few old ones still exist; they simply wore out from hard use and were replaced again and again as needed. Instead of covering just part of a room, as we often see today, floorcloths were usually stretched wall to wall and tacked in place over a bedding of straw strewn across the floor.

Techniques for decorating a floorcloth haven't changed much over the years. A coat of oil paint makes the canvas or sailcloth waterproof. Then a decorative design is painted on top that either is coordinated with or accents the room. A classic decorating technique is stenciling, along with painting that imitates marble, granite, or slate. Whimsical freehand motifs in lively colors work well on floorcloths, too. Brushing the finished cloth with several coats of nonyellowing polyurethane or varnish gives today's floorcloths the durability they lacked 200 years ago.

In an Arizona adobe home set high in red rock bluffs (above left), an oil-painted floorcloth frames an eighteenth-century scrub-top hutch table. In a Pennsylvania stone house (above right), the dining room's floorcloth has a stenciled motif that is repeated on the beams overhead.

In a 1960s Massachusetts ranch house remodeled to look old (opposite), the floorcloth provides a suitable setting for tea in the keeping room. (Directions to make this floorcloth are provided on page 152.)

A Hand-Painted Floorcloth

Did you ever wish you could have a small rug to match the pattern in your favorite vase? Or one that borrowed the colors from one fabric but the pattern from another? The solution is as easy as the necessary materials–some artist's canvas and acrylic paints.

Painted and decorated floors were very popular in the eighteenth century, and the floorcloth evolved as an economical, practical alternative to the more expensive carpets, tiles, and painted woods. For today's lifestyle, floorcloths provide portability, easy cleaning, and unlimited decorative potential.

Patterns can be painted freehand, traced, or stenciled. Straight lines can be made with a tape resist. Areas of spattered paint add textural interest, or try overlaying a marbleized background with a stencil pattern. Inspiration can come from fabric, wallpaper, china, artwork, even your flower garden.

DIRECTIONS

SIZE: 4' x 6' (1.2 x 1.8 m), or size as desired.

YOU WILL NEED: Extra-heavy artist's cotton canvas, available at art supply stores—2¼ yards (2.2 m), 60" (1.5 m) wide, or size of desired floorcloth, plus 2" (5.1 cm) extra all around; acrylic gesso; latex paint in background color (buff, as shown in photograph); acrylic paints in contrasting colors (navy and maroon, as shown); masking tape in ¾" (19-mm) width; matte or gel medium; white craft glue; water-based varnish and sealer; T square; yardstick; paint roller for flat, smooth surfaces; paint tray; 1" and 3" (25-mm and 76-mm) flat bristle brushes, 2" (51-mm) foam brush, and two ½" (13-mm) stencil brushes; chalk in a color to contrast with latex paint; rolling pin; stenciling supplies listed in general instructions on page 136.

PREPARING CANVAS: Using a pencil, yardstick, and T square, mark a 52" x 76" (132.1 x 193.1 cm) rectangle along the grain on the canvas. Cut out. Iron to eliminate any creases. Apply a smooth coat of gesso on one side (this will be the right side of the floorcloth) with a wide, flat bristle brush; let it dry.

PAINTING BACKGROUND COLOR: Using a paint roller, apply two coats of latex paint, letting each coat dry.

CREATING BORDERED BACKGROUND: With pencil and yardstick, measure and mark lines 2" (5.1 cm), 3½" (8.9 cm), 5" (12.7 cm), and 5¾" (14.6 cm) from edges all around. Apply tape along the outside of the outermost penciled rectangle, between the second and third rectangles, and to the inside of the innermost rectangle. Seal edges with a thin coat of matte medium to keep the paint from seeping under the tape. Using a narrow, flat brush, paint between pieces of the tape: Use one color (navy) to paint the wider, outer border, another color (maroon) for the narrow, inner border. Let dry; then apply a second coat for better coverage. Let dry before removing the tape.

MARKING PATTERN LINES: Measure to locate the exact center of the floorcloth. With colored chalk and T square, lightly mark a 5" (12.7-cm) square, perfectly centered, making sure its sides are parallel to the sides of the floorcloth. Divide the square diagonally in half in both directions, and extend these diagonals out to the border. Next, mark parallel diagonals from each corner of the square out to the border. Continue marking parallel diagonal lines in both directions, forming a 3½" (8.9-cm) grid over the entire floorcloth within the borders.

STENCILING: Following the general instructions trace the actual-size pattern on to a sheet of acetate (both colors are stenciled together). Cut out the four-petal and leaf motifs (do not cut out the crosses—these are registration marks to help you align the design properly). Place the stencil at the upper-left corner of the floorcloth, with each registration mark within a four-petal motif along an inter-

section of grid lines and each leaf motif centered on a diagonal line. Apply the paint with stencil brushes: Paint the petals one color (maroon), the leaves another (navy). Let dry. Lift the stencil and reposition it to the right, lining up the motifs in the same way. Repeat all the way to the right, and then end by stenciling just 2 of the four-petal motifs. Work the next row, using the top row of four petals for alignment only (they have been stenciled already at the bottom of the previous row). Continue until the whole floorcloth is completely stenciled.

FINISHING: Let the paint dry completely, then remove the chalk marks carefully with a damp cloth. Trim the floorcloth, leaving a 1″ (2.5-cm) border (buff-colored) from the edges all around. Cut diagonally across the corners up to the outer border. Turn the floorcloth over to the back, and using your finger, smooth white glue along the 1″ edge and fold down. Press the edges flat with a rolling pin. Let the glue dry, then turn the floorcloth back to the right side. Apply a thin coat of varnish sealer with a clean foam brush. Let it dry, then apply a second coat.

A Contemporary Stencil

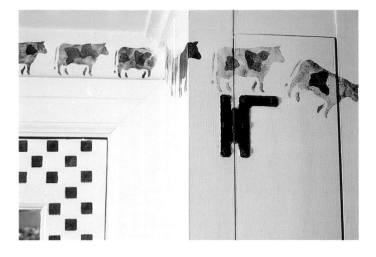

The art of stenciling reached its peak during the early 1800s, though the demand for stencils continued for about another 50 years. Professional stencilers abounded. Their patterns may have been charmingly naive, but their methods of laborious application with a piece of fabric were complex, requiring multiple stencils and shades of paint.

Today, stencil brushes and sponges make application a snap. This cow motif requires just two stencils and limited color, but the effects are humorously original.

DIRECTIONS

SIZE: Approximately 4″ (10 cm).

YOU WILL NEED: Black acrylic paint; ½″ (13 mm) stencil brush; additional stenciling supplies are listed in the general instructions on page 136.

MAKING STENCILS: Following the general instructions, cut at least 2 cow stencils, a stencil for both spots, and a stencil for each separate spot.

MARKING: To position the cows in a straight line, use a pencil and yardstick to lightly mark the guidelines on the wall or area to be stenciled. Here, the cows are positioned approximately ½″ apart; they also turn the corners and waver into a wide curve. If you prefer a more regular, even sequence, plan your spacing for the available area—or adjust the spacing between cows when you approach the end of the area to be stenciled. Planning ahead ensures you won't end up with partial motifs or a large space at the end of the available wall area.

STENCILING: Spray the adhesive on the wrong side of each stencil and let it dry. Follow the contemporary procedures outlined in the general instructions. The cows should be stenciled very lightly with a very dry brush for a pale gray, mottled effect. Occasionally, you may wish to apply paint more heavily to make an all-black cow.

To add the Holstein spots, leave the cow stencil in place after each light gray cow is stenciled—even after the paint is completely dry. Place 1 or 2 spot stencils on top of the cow stencil, and apply the black paint. To individualize the cows, vary the pattern of the spots: Center the spots or place them off center, use just 1 spot or the other or both, merge the spots, or turn them upside down or sideways. Let the paint dry; remove and separate the stencils for reuse.

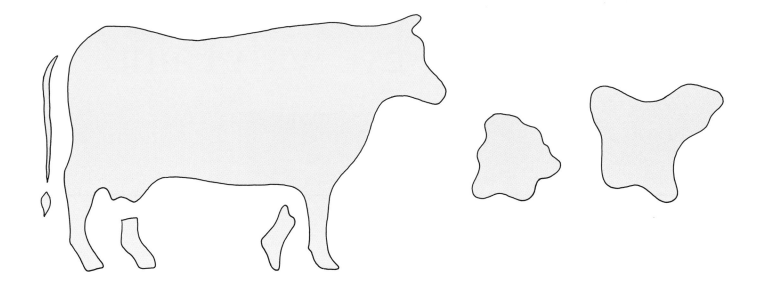

Fooling the Eye with Paint

Humor is as old as time. The painting technique known as *trompe l'oeil*, which is French for "fool the eye," is an example.

Trompe l'oeil has rural roots. The countryside and scenes from nature are familiar themes. As early as the fifteenth century, medieval artists were painting cloud-covered cathedral ceilings as if the roofs had been peeled back to reveal the star-filled heavens above, complete with inquisitive cherubs.

Today, *trompe l'oeil* continues to convey illusions. It is used to open the way to an imaginary world. Try embellishing a wall with a trailing vine, painting mice peeking out of pretend holes in the baseboards, lining up crockery on an imaginary shelf, or having a cow peering over the top of a Dutch door. Small rooms can be made to appear larger; large rooms can become more intimate or less imposing through *trompe l'oeil* effects.

Garlands of ivy, both stenciled and real, create a garden theme in a guest room (above left). Make-believe wisteria climbs the front of a cheerful pink playhouse (above right), while a pretend wreath tied with a bow decorates the door. When work crews unearthed eleven dishpans full of pottery shards and assorted treasures from beneath this restored eighteenth-century sea captain's house in New York (right), the owner repaired the items in her imagination and lined them up on a trompe l'oeil shelf in the kitchen. The makings of an Italian feast are realistically depicted on a kitchen wall (opposite below), as though they were sitting on the table. Clouds streak across the sky-blue ceiling of a screened porch (opposite above), where awning fabric cushions the wicker and shades the walls.

Wrapped in Scenery

In eighteenth- and nineteenth-century New England, itinerant artists roamed from town to town, painting murals on their customers' walls. One famous artist was Rufus Porter, who from 1824 until about 1845 painted his way from Maryland through New York, New Jersey, and Massachusetts, staying in taverns and homes along the way. For $10, he promised to complete four walls in five hours. Porter claimed his simple, highly stylized murals were better than wallpaper, which was "apt to get torn off" and also had the disadvantage of being "a resting place for various insects."

The owners of this 200-year-old New Hampshire house had Rufus Porter in mind when they asked artists David Wiggins and Joseph Swan to paint a mural in their bedroom, which was once the downstairs parlor. They felt the white walls needed warming up. Like the itinerants of centuries past, the artists lived with the owners as they did their work. It took three days of painting, sponging, stenciling, and freehand detailing to create the murals, which depict some of the owners' favorite things. Now the room is wrapped in scenery that evokes days gone by.

The murals in this master bedroom are recent, but they look as though they've always been a part of the 200-year-old house. After the walls were washed with color, the artists did the small wall (opposite) as a preview for the owners. Then, given the go-ahead, they proceeded to sponge, stencil, and hand-detail the walls with a 360-degree scenic view.

The fence on the wall over the bed (above) was typical of nineteenth-century artist Rufus Porter's work. A closeup view of the overmantel (right) depicts a house with a child in the window and a little girl playing with a hoop.

A Massachusetts family asked artist Sue Connell to paint their library walls (right) with a fantasy landscape. The murals accurately depict the Shaker simplicity of the house and the little barn across the road, although the barn has since been repainted and renovated for tenants. An-other portion of the mural (top) shows some of the animals the homeowners often observe congregating at their pond behind the vegetable garden—deer, rabbits, Canada geese, and all manner of birdlife.

A "High Country" Storyteller

Her enthusiasm is infectious. One meeting with Virginia McLaughlin and you'll be planning to have her paint her traditional murals on every wall of your house.

This dynamic painter didn't really set out to paint murals. McLaughlin was trained as a canvas artist, but her work has evolved through the years. She's been employed as a freelance mural artist and furniture painter and is often sought after for her expertise in graining, stenciling, and marbelizing. These days, painting murals in private homes and inns occupies much of her time.

Her work is done in the style of seventeenth- and eighteenth-century itinerant artists. A typical McLaughlin work features silhouettes of people playing with hoops or riding in stagecoaches and open wagons. The owners of the house may find themselves portrayed in Colonial dress doing chores or indulging in their favorite pastimes. McLaughlin describes her style as "high country"—"no ducks and chickens," she says determinedly.

The Mount Vernon Inn, in Alexandria, Virginia, located at the entrance gate to George Washington's home, features her work in its stately dining room. Here, senators frequently entertain foreign guests to give them a flavor of life in the early days of this country. McLaughlin's murals help tell the tale.

McLaughlin has devoted herself to restorations of all sorts. In 1975, she and her husband purchased their 1849 stone manor house. The fact that it had no heat, bathrooms, or running water did not deter them, and today the house is warm and livable. Using two original grained doors as her guide, McLaughlin grained 13 other doors in the house. Stenciled bedrooms and bathrooms, marbelized mantels and bathtubs, and stairway wall paintings in the house also attest to McLaughlin's skills.

The artist Virginia McLaughlin (*opposite above*) used her talents to decorate her 1850s stone house in Carroll Valley, Pennsylvania. She painted a landscape mural in the style of Rufus Porter (*right*). A collection of eighteenth- and nineteenth-century coverlets adorns the railing. A fireboard (*opposite below left*) depicts Carroll Valley landmarks; McLaughlin often incorporates a homeowner's family and local sites into commissioned works. The focal point of a painted windowshade (*opposite below right*) is the only covered bridge still used in Adams County, where the McLaughlins live.

Built by
Hand

The Legacy of Handcrafts

After all the major decorating is done—colors chosen, fabrics sewn—every room, be it humble or extravagant, requires a final touch. What it needs is a dose of humanity—the handcrafted items that bring any room to life. They have a quality that can't be matched by machine-made goods, whether one is comparing quilts, cookie jars, or rocking chairs. Besides, there's a special pleasure in being able to tell admirers, "I built it myself."

In earlier times, people made things by hand out of necessity. There were no nails, so wooden pegs were carved. If a chair was needed, you built one. Bowls were fashioned from the trunks of trees. Children's toys sprang from the fantasies of grandfathers who could whittle and aunts who could turn shriveled apples and cornhusks into dolls.

What people made depended largely on where they lived. New arrivals to this country searched the land for craft materials, and if what they'd known in their home-land wasn't available, they found acceptable substitutes. For instance, sheep tallow had always been used to make candles in England, but there were few sheep in the New World, so other animal fat had to be used at first. Colonialists made a happy and fragrant discovery when they found bayberries could be boiled to make wax.

Ingenuity was also fueled by remembrance. Swedes in Delaware and Germans in Pennsylvania built America's first log cabins based on dwellings they'd known in their homeland. If a gameboard hadn't been squeezed into a family's belongings for the trip across the ocean, new ones were carved for a family's amusement as they gathered around the fire at night.

Today, handcrafted items that have survived the years tell much about their makers. And items newly made in the old tradition carry on the legacy for generations to come. Today's artisans are crafting tomorrow's antiques. Our only obligation is to carry them safely into the future, as our ancestors did for us.

Displayed on the breakfast porch of a 1923 Georgian stone house in Virginia is part of the owners' collection of 50 antique birdhouses. Abandoned birds' nests are clustered around a fanciful tin-roofed log cabin with a stone foundation, newly made as a whimsy by a local stonemason. The smaller cabin is a bark birdhouse, also new. The airy porch has proven ideal for drying delphinium, lamb's ears, yarrow, and other garden herbs and flowers. Some hang from a worn ladder, while others are suspended from an old iron hook once used to haul coal miners' laundry up a mine shaft. The heart-shaped grapevine wreath is embellished with autumn leaves, boxwood, and juniper from the yard, as well as tin cutouts bought at a country fair.

Toys and Small Dwellings

Old-fashioned toys and small dwellings are nostalgic reminders of childhood. Beside their obvious charm, these items conjure up a time of innocence and wonder.

The fascination for little things is not reserved for the young. On the contrary, adults gravitate toward these symbols of yesteryear. Entire collections have been built around beloved rag dolls, dollhouse furniture, rattles, tops, pull toys, and carved beasts like cows, pigs, and rabbits.

Most Colonial toys for boys were fashioned from scraps of wood that were transformed in the hands of a whittler into blocks, boats, or tops. For girls, clothespin dolls were common, as were rag dolls and old-time stuffed animals—pets made from quilt or fabric scraps.

In the early 1900s, miniature villages were popular Pennsylvania-Dutch Christmas decorations, sometimes made from cigar boxes. Small-scale wooden villages were also carved from blocks of wood and hand-painted to create realistic street scenes. Today, the holidays may not seem complete without one of these little communities resting atop the mantelpiece.

Birdhouses are popular, too, if they're not currently occupied by feathered tenants. Eager collectors snap them up as decorative accents for their homes. Or if you'd rather attract birds to your home, you can build a birdhouse from the project on page 170.

On a chimney cupboard in a Texas farmhouse (above) stands a row of turn-of-the-century squeak toys; open a door and a rooster pops out and crows. A graceful duo (right) hand-carved by a New England artisan poses on a kitchen cupboard newly made of wainscoting.

A pleasing still life, created from the most ordinary objects, can be set up anywhere. Take the little blue-and-white birdhouse lined up in a row of geraniums and marigolds in identical pots (above) on the knee-high ledge of a patio on Fire Island in New York. According to the owner, an arrangement like this might last for an entire summer, a month, or just a week, depending on her whims, how the flowers fare, and whether or not the birdhouse attracts tenants, which seems to depend largely on the cats in the neighborhood. During the nineteenth century, German toy villages like this one (right) were popular; handmade replicas are common today.

A Simple Birdhouse

Birds bring added pleasure to any backyard, terrace, or patio. Not only do they provide hours of interesting watching, their songs gladden the heart. It is important to remember when building your own birdhouse that the type you make determines the kind of birds you attract. Of the three basic shapes of birdhouses the most popular, and the type shown here and on the top of page 169, is the hanging birdhouse that wrens prefer. There are also mounted houses for bluebirds and swallows and roofed nesting shelves for robins.

Make sure your birdhouse has enough ventilation and drainage holes. Additional modifications to keep in mind are height, floor size, opening size, and position. Also, be sure to build it for easy cleaning after a nesting family has left. Otherwise you will not attract new birds.

DIRECTIONS

SIZE: Approximately 8½" (22 cm) high.

YOU WILL NEED: 1 x 6 pine, 1½' (137.2-cm) length for walls; ¼" (6-mm) plywood for base and roof (refer to figure); ¼" dowel, 2" (5.1-cm) length; 1⅛" (28.6-mm) finishing nails; 1" (25-mm) wood screws; wood glue; small cans of white primer and oil-base paint in white and blue (or colors as desired); sandpaper; rotary saw or jigsaw; drill with ¹⁄₁₆", ⅛", ¼", and 1¼" (1.6- to 31.7-mm) bits; hammer; screwdriver; 1" flat paintbrushes.

CUTTING: Using good-quality pine, mark and cut a front and back to the outer dimensions shown in the figure, plus 2 sides measuring 4" x 5¼" (10.2 x 13.3 cm). Use a 45° angle to cut roof peaks on the front and back. From plywood, cut a roof section 4½" x 6½" (11.4 x 16.5 cm), another 4¾" x 6½" (12.1 x 16.5 cm), and a base 6½" square.

PREPARING THE PIECES: Carefully sand all rough edges smooth. On the front, measure down 3¼" (8.3 cm) from the peak of the roof and mark a dot. Drill a 1¼" (3.2-cm) hole at the mark for the entrance. Mark a dot 1" (2.5 cm) below the hole and centered between the sides; drill a ¼" (6-mm) hole for the perch. Drill several ⅛" (3-mm) holes near the top of each side for ventilation and also in the floor for drainage.

JOINING PIECES: Apply glue on the adjoining edges. Space the nails and screws evenly. First assemble the walls: Glue the sides flush with the side edges of the front and back. Hammer the nails from the front and back into the sides. For the perch, apply glue to the end of the dowel and insert into the ¼" hole.

PAINTING: Prime all exterior wall surfaces and all plywood surfaces. Paint all surfaces with two coats of paint, letting them dry after each coat. Paint the roof blue and everything else white.

ADDING THE ROOF: Apply glue to the top edges of the birdhouse on one side only. Place the slightly shorter roof section on that side, beginning at the top peaks, and make sure the top edge is flush with the slope on the other side. The side edges should extend equally beyond the front and back of the birdhouse. Hammer two nails, evenly spaced, through the roof into the front peak, and another two nails through the roof into the back peak. Glue the larger roof section over the other side of the front and back peaks, overlapping the edge of the previous roof section. Nail in place as before.

ADDING THE BASE: Center the birdhouse on the base and trace around it lightly in pencil. Measuring carefully, mark and drill four ¹⁄₁₆" (1.6-mm) pilot holes all the way through the base, positioning them so that two screws may go through the holes and penetrate the bottom edges of each side of the birdhouse. Replace the base, and putting your pencil through the drilled holes, mark dots on the bottom edges of the sides. Drill pilot holes in the sides at the marked dots. Secure the base to the house with screws. Avoid gluing the bottom in place; you should be able to remove it for cleaning.

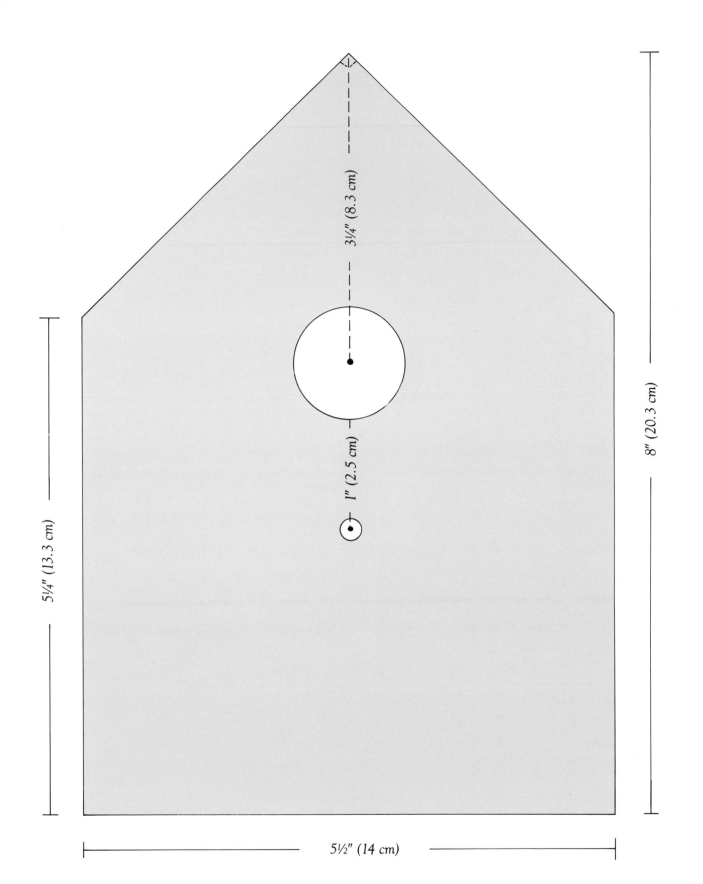

3¼" (8.3 cm)

1" (2.5 cm)

8" (20.3 cm)

5¼" (13.3 cm)

5½" (14 cm)

Gameboards ~ Simple Country Pleasures

Gameboards turn heads whenever they show their faces. Hung alone, a gameboard can be as arresting as a fine painting or quilt. When hung in groups, each addition enhances the whole collection.

Most gameboards are square or rectangular; a few are miniature. Some are pictorial, embellished with the sun, moon, stars, or scenes from nature. A gameboard often tells a story: The family name may be carved on the back, along with the date or place where the board was made, and to discover which games were played, just look at how the paint has worn. Two-sided gameboards show the thrifty nature of our forefathers; putting Parcheesi on one side and Backgammon on the other made the most of one piece of wood.

Gameboards remind us of the days when families relaxed together pursuing simple pleasures. Gambling may have been frowned on by some of the more puritanical Colonists, but a rousing game of checkers was always welcomed.

It's easy to replicate the antique look of a gameboard (see the project on page 174). Well-made reproductions can still convey a warm country feeling.

A *collection of nineteenth-century gameboards decorates a hallway (below left). A turn-of-the-century rocking horse is silhouetted against a backdrop of gameboards (below right). The* *blanket chest it stands on is thought to have been made in New England or Pennsylvania. Checkerboards in their many guises (opposite) are newly made to look old.*

A Checkers Gameboard

The game of checkers can be dated back to A.D. 1000 in France. Traveling across both land and time, the game changed from the French *jeu force* to English draughts to American checkers. In fact, our hard-working ancestors relied on checkers and Parcheesi for a chance to play and relax.

Boards for these games were most often homemade. They ranged from very simple, rustic designs to highly imaginative ones with elaborate borders or painted motifs. Both types are highly collectible today. Their warm colors and soft patinas make gameboards a folk art worthy of display on any wall.

DIRECTIONS

SIZE: 19½″ x 29″ (49.5 x 73.7 cm).

YOU WILL NEED: ¾″ (19.1-mm) pine or plywood cut to an 18″ x 27½″ (45.7 x 69.9 cm) rectangle; wood molding or firring strips: 1 x 1 with rounded edge, 3′(.9-m) length; 1 x 2, 8′(2.4-m) length; wood glue; 1″ (25-mm) finishing nails; oil-base paint in white and yellow (or colors as desired); turpentine; clear, matte-finish varnish; 1½″ (38-mm) masking tape; matte gel medium (optional); clear acrylic spray; pencil; ruler; sandpaper; rag; tack cloth; handsaw; hammer; 2″ (51-mm) flat paintbrush; large tin cans for diluting paint and cleaning brushes.

CUTTING PIECES: From 1 x 1 round-edge molding, cut two 18″ (45.7-cm) strips. From 1 x 2 strips, cut two 27½″ (69.9-cm) lengths and two 19½″ (49.5-cm) lengths. Sand all the pieces lightly and wipe with a tack cloth.

"PICKLING" WOOD: Thin the white paint with turpentine. Apply the paint with a flat brush to the wood surface, stroking along the grain, and then immediately wipe off the excess with a rag. Let it dry. Repeat on all surfaces of all wood pieces.

PAINTING CHECKERBOARD: Choose the better surface of the pine or plywood rectangle for the game board surface. Spray this with clear acrylic sealer.

Position the board with the shorter dimension across and the longer up and down. Carefully measure and lightly pencil a horizontal line across the center of the board. Repeat with a vertical center line, but stop the line 4¾″ (12.1 cm) from the short edges of the board. Lay 1½″ masking tape across the board, with the first strip just below the penciled horizontal line. Working downward, begin covering the surface with horizontal rows of tape. Take care that the edges of the tape just touch. After placing the first three rows, lift up the second strip of tape and place it below the third to form the fourth row. Add a fifth row, and then lift up the same strip of tape as before and place it under the fifth strip. Add a seventh row, and again remove the strip just above it. In the same way, work above the first strip for seven rows, removing alternate strips to keep subsequent lengths of tape exactly 1½″ apart.

Press down the edges of the remaining tape tightly to the surface. Beginning at the vertical center line, repeat the process with vertical rows of tape to the side edges. It may make it easier to work if you turn the board so that the long sides are at the top and bottom and you can work in the same way as before. Apply matte gel medium to the tape edges or spray it with clear acrylic and let it dry. This will prevent paint from seeping under the edges of the tape and result in crisper, cleaner-looking checks.

Paint the exposed areas using a flat paintbrush and one coat of contrasting color paint (here bright yellow); stroke on paint along the grain of the wood. Let it dry and then remove the tape. Spray it with sealer and let it dry. Place the tape, first horizontally, then vertically, over each row that contains previously painted blocks. Press the edges

tightly to the surface and then spray it with acrylic or apply matte gel medium. Paint the areas that are now exposed in the same way as before. Let it dry, remove the tape, and touch up the checked design as necessary.

ASSEMBLING THE GAMEBOARD: First, glue the flat edge of the rounded molding to both ends of the checkerboard square to define the areas for captured checkers. Glue the longer 1 x 2 strips to the long edges of the board to form a border. Hammer nails into each side: into the center of each rounded molding strip, then, directly below those nails into the board. Glue the shorter 1 x 2 strips along the short edges of the checkerboard to complete the border. Hammer the nails into the board and into the longer strips, spacing them equally.

FINISHING: For a worn or antiqued look, sand it lightly to remove some of the paint. Apply two coats of varnish, letting the piece dry and sanding after each coat.

Ornamental Tin

For a distinctive look in any room, try tin. Tin chandeliers and pie-plate sconces have lit country houses for centuries. A row of tin canisters completes a homey kitchen. What's an antique sideboard without punched tin doors? Tin can be cut, punched, hammered, and crimped with marvelous results, and it has a wholesome, earthy look.

Tinsmithing crossed the ocean from England. White-smiths (as they were known to distinguish them from blacksmiths) often peddled their wares from wagons rattling with baking pans, Bible boxes, cups, pails, candlesticks, teapots, coffee pots, and watering cans. Toleware was the most decorative and expensive tin, its black background frequently stenciled or handpainted with a wide array of colorful designs.

Newly crafted punched tin panels embellish kitchen cupboard doors (above). This patriotic pie safe (right) is a family heirloom that's at least 100 years old. The eagle was a popular decorative symbol during the nineteenth century. Tin insets in cupboard doors add a distinctive, old-time warmth to a country kitchen (opposite).

A Tenderness for Tin

Carrying on a centuries-old American tradition, metalsmith Ivan Barnett imbues his craft with a contemporary playfulness. A resident of Lancaster County, Pennsylvania—home of the Amish community—Barnett draws on a wide variety of sources as inspiration for his work.

Although Barnett studied advertising and illustration in art school, he switched to metalwork when he got out of the army. He had always had a great affinity for working with his hands. "I pursued the effects I wanted to achieve through experimentation," he explains. "My initial interest was to learn how traditional metalwork was done, and I studied with blacksmiths and visited museums." His goal, rather than doing strict reproductions, was to create what he calls "inspirations."

Working out of a 3,500-square-foot contemporary barn, Barnett draws on a varied repertoire of folk art for his designs, which he produces as collections, limited-quantity pieces, and one-of-a-kind commissions. His first collections were inspired by animal motifs found in historical objects produced in Pennsylvania-Dutch country, such as windmill weights, weather vanes, and tin practice targets. Now his latest designs are animal and figurative forms related to Central and South American folk art and legends.

The artist is surrounded by a variety of his whimsical lightweight metal designs (above). To ornament the metal rabbit (opposite top), artist Ivan Barnett applied water-based paint to allow the oxided, irregular surface to show through. A collage of horses, roosters, and early-morning sunbursts (opposite below left) evokes the bucolic feeling of Lancaster County, Pennsylvania, where the artist lives. Barnett creates variations in the horses' coats with an oxidation process that weathers the metal. Hefty cows sport dainty hand-painted flowers riveted to the metal in the traditional manner (opposite below right).

Most of his designs are produced in oxidized steel, yet the shapes, colors, and sizes are always changing. Water-based paints that allow the natural textures to show through are applied, and the metal silhouettes are often ornamented with wood. The processes of painting, sanding, and assembling the artwork are all done in the barn, and the individual metal pieces are attached and applied through iron riveting. Notes Barnett, "I'm keeping elements of the tradition in the process."

His enthusiasm for handcrafted materials has led Barnett to immerse himself in every step of his art. In his early metal assemblages, Barnett used old barn roofing and rusted scraps of tin. Now, because it is difficult to obtain old metal, the artist ages new materials himself. Barnett favors a natural approach to aging metal because it is ecologically sound and achieves the time-worn texture of genuine old metal.

The chairs on an Adirondack porch (above) afford a mountain view in America's largest state park. Rush-seated rockers with rush or slatted backs are typical in this part of New York State and throughout New England and the South. The chair in the middle offers a reclining perspective by day and a view of the star-filled heavens at night. Twig "Mom and Pop" chairs, constructed of willow with sturdy maple bases (left), were handmade by their Michigan owners, who earn their living from this craft. Of older vintage is the graceful twig chair (opposite) that stands in dramatic counterpoint to the arrowhead-motif shutters outside this Adirondack camp. Deep green and brick red colors are favored in this neck of the woods.

Rustic Chairs

When stools grew backs and turned into chairs, the scene was set for relaxation. What one sits on depends on where one lives and often what one is wearing. For instance, the wide skirts of yesteryear inspired the armless chair in France. In 1904, an inventor in Westport, New York, patented the Adirondack chair, which evolved into the comfortable slatted outdoor chair we are familiar with today.

Rocking chairs were an English inspiration that became popular all across America. In mountainous areas, rustic and imaginative chairs were assembled from twigs during long, cold winters. The craft is still alive today.

Those who haunt flea markets and estate sales may find that old chair frames, missing their seats and in need of attention, possess a sculptural elegance that demands restoration. The frames can be polished and new seats woven with tape (see the woven chair seat project on page 182). Then chairs are as good as new for sitting—or hang them from a pegboard in the Shaker tradition to show off their great good looks.

A Woven Chair Seat

Wonderful chairs can be found in antique or junk stores or at flea markets, but often their seats are worn or broken. It's very easy to repair an upholstered seat that is attached to the base by screws underneath, but it is a bit more complex to repair caning, rushing, or woven seats. If your chair has a seat that is fastened by rungs (sometimes also called rails), then replacing the seat with a simple tape-woven covering is an easy job.

This chair seat is based on ones commonly found on Shaker chairs, but it is suitable for a large number of antique chair types from rockers to ladderback chairs, as well as many contemporary wooden chairs.

DIRECTIONS

YOU WILL NEED: Any chair whose seat is supported on rungs; 1″ (25-mm) chair tapes in black and red or colors as desired (see chart; contact Shaker Workshops for materials); carpet tacks; 1″ foam pad cut to fit area defined by rungs; scissors; hammer; blunt knife, screwdriver, or spoon.

DETERMINING YARDAGE: To determine the approximate yardage required to make replacement chair seats, find the seat size closest to yours in the chart below, adding or subtracting a few yards as required. The following yardage is for one color. For a two-color checkerboard design, you will need half the amount for each color.

Size of seat		Tape	
Inches	Cm	Yards	Meters
13 x 10	33 x 25.4	14	12.8
15 x 12	38.1 x 30.5	20	18.3
18 x 14	45.7 x 35.6	20	18.3
19 x 16	48.3 x 40.6	33	30.2
21 x 17	53.3 x 43.2	38	34.7
22 x 19	55.9 x 48.3	42	38.4

SPLICING: Tape comes in prewound rolls of 5 yards (4.6 m) and 10 yards (9.1 m), which have been found to be convenient weaving lengths. If you happen to reach the end of a piece of tape before completing either the warping or the weaving, it will be necessary to splice it: Sew the overlapping ends of the tapes together firmly and make sure that the splice falls on the underside of the woven seat.

WARPING: The first step in seating the chair is known as "warping." This simply entails wrapping tape around the front and back rungs to provide a warp both on the top and the bottom of the seat (figure 1 on page 184). The chair shown in the photograph features a navy blue warp and a white weft. If you plan to weave with two colors of tape, use the darker color for the warp.

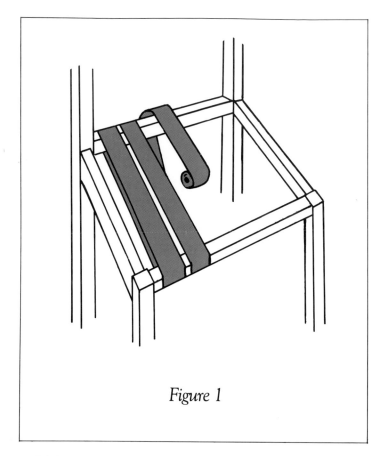

Figure 1

To begin warping, fold 1″ of tape under at one end. Use one or two tacks to tack both layers of this end firmly to the inner side of the back rung as close as possible to the left back post. The doubled-over end will point toward the top of the chair. Bring the coil of tape behind and over the back rung and forward to the front rung, at right angles to both the front and back rungs. Bring it over the front rung and return it to the back rung, taking it under and then over the back rung, and then bring it back to the front. Make sure that the tape does not get twisted. Continue in this way until you reach the back right post and there is no space for another warp on the back rung (there will, however, be extra space at either side on the front rung). Then bring the tape over and under the front rung and back to the back rung. Leaving an extra 2″ (5.1 cm) of tape, cut off the excess. Before this end is tacked in place, it is important to pull out as much slack in the warping as possible. However, the tape should not be stretched so tight that it causes the front rung to bow, though it should be firm. Check also that the tape runs at right angles to the front and back rungs. Fold the end

under and securely tack it to the bottom right of the back rung, where it will overlap the last warp strip.

Because the side rungs are splayed in the front on most chairs, there will probably be a triangular-shaped area on either side of the seat, which will be without warps; these warps will be added at a later stage.

SECURING THE WEFT: Using the coil of tape that will be the weft, fold 1″ of the end under and tack it to the inside of the left side rung as close as possible to the left back post. The folded end will be pointing up. Insert the pad before weaving the weft.

INSERTING THE PAD: Stuff the pad, which has been cut to fill the seat area, between the top and bottom levels of the warping. While a pad is not essential, it will help prevent sagging and the effects of excessive wear. Since the pad maintains contact between the two layers, the lower layer can help support the weight of the sitter, which would otherwise be carried only by the upper layer of tape.

WEAVING: Bring the free end of the coil of tape around and over the left side rail and continue under the first warp strip of the top layer. Then bring the end over the next warp strip, under one, over one, and so on, until you reach

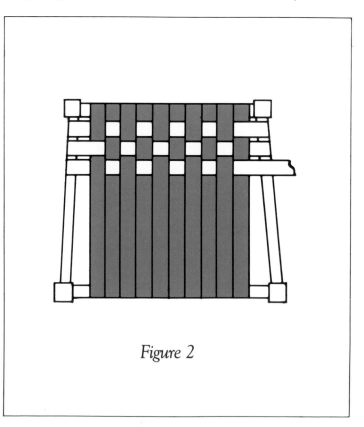

Figure 2

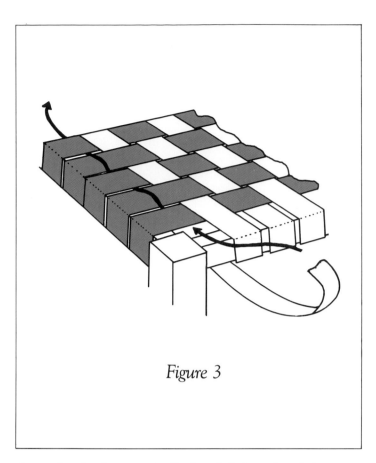

Figure 3

the right back post. Pull the full length of the tape through the top layer of warp strips. Bring the tape over and around the side rung. Turn the chair over and repeat the process on the lower layer of warp strips. Next, weave the weft again through the top layer of warp strips, this time starting over the first strip, under the second, and so on. If your warp and weft are different colors, you will start to see a checkerboard pattern emerge (figure 2). Again turn the chair over and return the weft through the lower level of warp strips so as to form the start of a checkerboard pattern, as on the top layer.

NOTE: At the right side of the chair, the end warp of the bottom layer (which has been tacked to the right side of the back rung) will somewhat overlap the second to the last warp on the same side. It is essential that these two be treated as a single warp; that is, the weft must be carried over or under both of them together. Only in this way can a checkerboard pattern be created on the bottom of the seat; in the finished seat, this inconsistency will not be noticeable.

Continue weaving in a checkerboard pattern until the weft reaches the front posts of the chair. Always make sure that the tape does not twist. Pull it firmly each time it is brought through the warp strips and keep the rows as straight as possible, each touching the last. The final row on the top of the seat will abut the front posts on the side rungs and should curve slightly toward the front rung to keep the warps smooth and flat. Since at this point the warp will be tight, a blunt knife, screwdriver, or the handle of a metal spoon will be useful for lifting the warp strips to permit the weft to pass under them. Cut the weft long enough to end on the bottom of the chair, fold 1" of the end under, and tack it to the left side rung as close as possible to the left front post. (If there is not sufficient room to weave it through to the left side of the chair, tack it to the bottom of the front rung.)

HANDLING THE FRONT CORNERS: The final step is filling in the corners of the seat with added warps. One additional warp—or sometimes two or three, depending on the size and type of the chair—will be required on either side of the seat to fill out the warping near the front posts. Putting in these warps demands care. First, cut 2 strips of tape the same color as the warp to a length that will allow them to run from the front rung to the back rung on both the top and the bottom of the seat (that is, double the depth of the chair), plus 2"-3" (5.1-7.6 cm). Weave them in parallel to the last warp on either side of the top of the seat, maintaining the checkerboard pattern. Bring them over the front rung, and similarly weave them in on the bottom (figure 3).

Because of the triangular shape of the areas to be filled in, these warps cannot be carried all the way to the back posts of the chair but should be woven through the wefts until they meet the side rungs. Tuck their ends under the wefts and secure them, either by tacking to the side rungs (under a weft, which may be lifted with a blunt knife) or by carefully gluing them to the bottom of the weft with cloth glue.

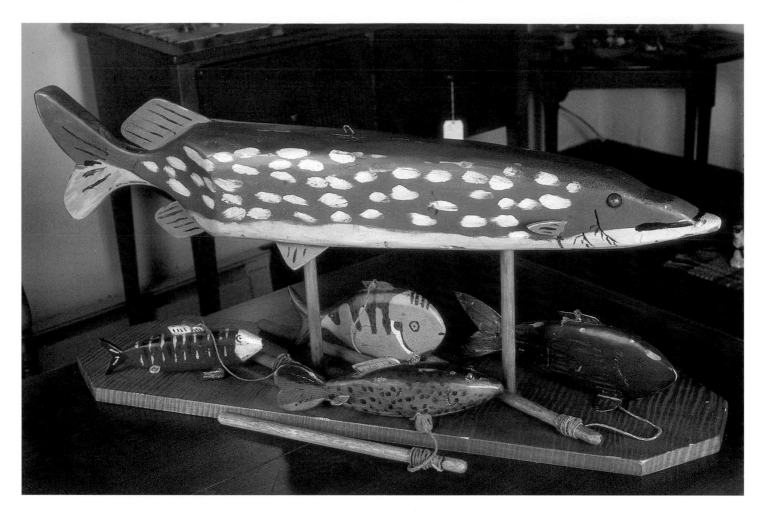

Handpainted fish decoys (above) carved by David's son Jason lure fish—and collectors—as successfully as their antique counterparts. Furniture salesmen used to travel with tiny versions of their firms' wares to give customers a first-hand look (left). Today, the workshops' studios do the same job by sending photographs of their work through the mail. David T. Smith (opposite) weaves cattails into a rush seat for one of his reproduction side chairs.

An Artisan in Wood

Tucked away on five wooded acres in southwestern Ohio is the farm where David T. Smith grew up. The cluster of buildings, which looks like a small village from yesteryear, are now his workshops and showrooms. Here, Smith and his staff of 45 craftspeople reproduce classic American country furniture, lighting, chairs, pottery, and hand-forged iron.

The workshops operate much like an old-fashioned guild. Each piece is painstakingly crafted with care, and time and attention are lavished on every detail. A single piece of furniture is put together from start to finish by only one or two people. Dovetailed or mortise-and-tenon joints and hand-carved pegs are the norm. Finishes are applied with goose feathers, combs, and fingertips in the colors favored by Early American artisans.

Smith's pottery company, Turtlecreek Potters, turns out reproductions of English delftware, and American and European redware pottery. Its line of redware, based on The Henry Ford Museum's collections, wear a traditional lead glaze. These display pieces are fired in an outdoor wood-burning kiln that gives the pottery shadings of color that don't appear when modern-day electric kilns are used.

Smith started his enterprise in 1980, after many years of making furniture for himself and restoring antique pieces. In addition to making a regular line of furniture, the workshops can custom make almost anything from the period 1700 to 1850, from William and Mary to Sheraton.

Today, Smith's whole family is involved in the business, which has grown steadily. What began as a modest operation has burgeoned into a thriving enterprise, while carefully retaining its flavor of the past.

Resources

CRAFTSPEOPLE PROFILED IN THIS BOOK

Ivan Barnett
The Patina Gallery
131 W. Palace Avenue
Santa Fe, NM 87501
505.986.3432
www.patina-gallery.com
Fine hand-crafted jewelry and contemporary crafts

Sue Connell
The Clayton Store
The Canaan-Southfield Road
Southfield, MA 01259
413.229.2621
Stenciler, muralist

Elizabeth Eakins
21 East 65th Street
New York, NY 10021
212.628.1950
Custom-crafted rugs

The Foltz Pottery
225 North Pear Town Road
Reinholds, PA 17569
www.foltzpottery.com
Potter

Virginia Jacobs McLaughlin
303 Fleming Avenue
Frederick, MD 21701
301.696.0606
Specializing in 18th & 19th Century wall paintings

David T. Smith
3600 Shawham Road
Morow, OH 45152
513.932.2472
www.davidtsmith.com
Woodworker

POTTERY, TABLEWARE

J.K. Adams Co.
1430 Route 30
Dorset, VT 05251
800.451.6118
www.jkadams.com
Wooden bowls, boards

Beaumont Brothers Pottery
315 East Main Street
Crookville, OH 43731
740.982.0055
Stoneware

Bennington Potters
324 County Street
Bennington, VT 05201
802.447.7531
Earthenware, spatterware

DRIED FLOWERS, WREATHS

Delicate Designs
59 Kenmore Avenue
Amherst, NY 14226
800.PINK.HSE
www.delicatedesignsflorist.com
Wreaths and arrangements

Faith Mountain Company
P.O. Box 199
12625 Lee Hwy
Sperryville, VA 22740
800.822.7238
www.faithmountain.com
Wreaths, bouquets

San Francisco Herb Company
250 14th Street
San Francisco, CA 94103
415.861.7174
www.sfherb.com
Potpourri kits

Betsy Williams
155 Chestnut Street
Andover, MA 01810
978.470.0911
www.betsywilliams.com
Wreaths, arrangements, potpourri, and weddings

NEEDLEWORK

American Crewel & Canvas
7373 Zion Church Road
Parsonsburg, MD 21849
410.749.0394
Crewel kits

Country Stitching
P. O. Box 119
Willow Grove, PA 19090
215.885.5656
Sampler kits

The Stitchery
120 North Meadows Road
Medfield, MA 02052
508.359.7702
www.thestitchery.com
Cross-stitch, knitting supplies

TEXTILES, FIBERS

Chicago Weaving Corp.
5900 Northwest Highway
Chicago, IL 60631
773.631.0200
Homespun table linens, throws

The Fiber Studio
9 Foster Hill Road
P. O. Box 637
Henniker, NH 03242-0637
www.fiberstudio.com
Yarns, spinning equipment

Jamie Harmon
RD 2 Box 170-150K
Richmond, VT 05477
Homespun and naturally dyed wool yarns

Mystic Valley Traders
4-B Henshaw Street
Woburn, MA 01801
800.922.0660
www.mysticvaly.com
Bedcoverings, throws

Northampton Wools
11 Pleasant Street
Northampton, MA 01060
413.586.4331
Yarns, patterns

Paper White
P.O. Box 956
Fairfax, CA 94930
415.457.7673
White cutwork, lace-trimmed bed linens

The Seraph-West
5606 E. State Rd, Route 37
Delaware, OH 43015
800.737.2742
www.theseraph.com
Custom-crafted furniture

Park B. Smith
295 Fifth Avenue
New York, NY 10016
212.889.1818
www.pbsltd.com
Homespun linens, pillows

Joan Toggitt Ltd.
2 Riverview Drive
Somerset, NJ 08873
732.562.8888
www.zweigart.com
Zweigart fabrics

The Weaver's Knot
508 Inlet Drive
Seneca, SC 29601
800.680.7747
Fibers and dyestuffs

QUILTING

Dorr Mill Store
P.O. Box 88, Hale Street
Guild, NH 03754
603.863.1197
www.dorrmillstore.com
Rug wool and cotton fabric

Hinterberg Design Inc.
2805 E. Progress Drive
West Bend, WI 53095
800.443.5800
www.hinterberg.com
Quilting frames and hoops

Keepsake Quilting
P. O. Box 1618
Centre Harbor, NH 03226
800.525.8086
www.keepsakequilting.com
Quilt patterns, quilts, stencils

Quilts Unlimited
440A Duke of Gloucester
Williamsburg, VA 23185
757.253.8700
www.quiltsunlimited.com
Quilts, handcrafts

FIBER PUBLICATIONS

American Quilter
American Quilter's Society
P. O. Box 3290
Paducah, KY 42002
270.898.7903
www.aqsquilt.com

Fiberarts
50 College Street
Asheville, NC 28801
800.284.3388

Quilter's Newsletter Magazine
P. O. Box 59021
Boulder, CO 80332-9021
800.477.6089
www.quilts-online.com/qnm

Rug Hooking
P. O. Box 15760
Harrisburg, PA 17110
800.233.9055

Shuttle, Spindle & Dyepot
Handweavers Guild
3327 Duluth Highway, #201
Duluth, GA 30136-3373
770.495.7702
www.weavespindye.org

FLOORCOVERINGS

Capel, Inc.
P.O.Box 826
831 North Main Street
Troy, NC 27371
800.334.3711
www.capelrugs.com
Braided, hooked, and rag rugs

1840 House
237 Pine Point Road
Scarborough, ME 04074
207.883.5403
Over 200 designs, kits, supplies

Great Northern Rug Weaving
Suppliers
P. O. Box 462
451 East D Avenue
Kalamazoo, MI 49004
616.341.9752
Cotton & wool rugs, equipment

McAdoo Rugs
P.O. Box 847
The Red Mill
N. Bennington, VT 05257
802.442.3563
www.mcadoorugs.com
Hooked rugs

Mills River Industries
713 Old Orchard Road
Hendersonville, NC 28739
704.687.9778
Braided rugs

Joan Moshimer Studio
W. Cushing and Co.
21 North Street
P.O. Box 351
Kennebunkport, ME 04046
800.626.7847
www.wcushing.com
All rug-hooking supplies

Mulberry Street Rugs
21655 Circle Trail
Topanga, CA 90290
310.455.3995
Braided rugs

Yankee Pride
29 Parkside Circle
Braintree, MA 02188
800.848.7610
www.yankee-pride.com
Rag, hooked and braided rugs

PAINTERS

David Wiggins
Joseph Swann
5 York Street
Nantucket, MA 02554
Muralists, spongers, stencilers

PAINTS, STENCILING

Gail Grisi Stenciling
P.O. Box 1263-H
Haddonfield, NJ 08033
856.354.1757
www.gailgrisistenciling.com
*Pre-cut, ready-to-use
stencils, stenciling supplies*

Ivy Crafts Imports
P. O. Box 887
Riverdale, MD 20738
301.474.7347

Old Fashioned Milk Paint
Company
P.O. Box 222
Groton, MA 01450
978.448.6336
www.milkpaint.com
Milk paints

Stencil House of New
Hampshire
P.O. Box 16109
Hooksett, NH 03106
800.622.9416
www.stencilhouse.com
Stencils

Texas Art Supply
2001 Montrose
Houston, TX 77006
713.526.5221
www.texasart.com
Paints

HARDWARE, WOOD CRAFTS

Country Accents
P.O. Box 437
Montoursville, PA 17754
570.478.4127
www.piercedtin.com
Punched tin panels

Historic Housefitters Co.
509 Route 312, PO Box 26
Brewster, NY 10509
800.247.4111
www.historichousefitters.com
*Wrought iron hardware,
handmade lighting*

The Renovator's Supply
Millers Fall, MA 01349
800.659.2211
Hardware, plumbing, lighting

Virginia Metalcrafters
1010 East Main Street
P.O. Box 1068
Waynesboro, VA 22980
540.949.9400
www.vametal.com
*Brass hardware, garden
products, fireplace, lighting*

Walnut Hollow Farm
1409 State Road 23
Dodgeville, WI 53533
800.950.5101
www.walnuthollow.com
Natural woodcrafts

FURNITURE

Amish Country Collection
P. O. Box 271, Sunset Valley
New Castle, PA 16105
724.458.4811
Willow and slat furniture

Great Meadows Joinery
85 Main Street
Concord, MA 01742
978.287.5955
www.greatmeadowsjoinery.com
*Custom-made Shaker
reproductions*

Reed Brothers
5000 Turner Road
Sepastopol, CA 95472
707.795.6261
*Handcarved redwood furniture
for garden & home*

Shaker Workshops
18 Mill Lane
Arlington, MA 02476
800.840.9121
www.shakerworkshops.com
Shaker-style furniture

Photography Credits

2	Keith Scott Morton	32	Keith Scott Morton
4–5	Jessie Walker		(left and below
6	Jon Elliott		right)
	(above left)		Jessie Walker
	Paul Kopelow		(above right)
	(above right)	33	Paul Nystrom
	Keith Scott Morton	35	Keith Scott Morton
	(below)	36	Doug Kennedy
7	Jessie Walker	37	Jessie Walker
	(above left)		(above and below)
	Frank W. Ockenfels	38	André Gillardin
	3rd (above right)	39	André Gillardin
	Keith Scott Morton	40–41	Keith Scott Morton
	(below left)	42	Lynn Karlin
	André Gillardin	44	Jessie Walker
	(below right)	45	Paul Kopelow
8	Keith Scott Morton	48	Paul Kopelow
10	Keith Scott Morton		(above)
12	Jessie Walker		Keith Scott Morton
13	Jessie Walker		(below)
14–15	Keith Scott Morton	49	Keith Scott Morton
17	Keith Scott Morton	50	Chris Mead
18	Paul Kopelow	52	Keith Scott Morton
19	Doug Kennedy	53	Jessie Walker
	(above left and	54	Keith Scott Morton
	right)	56	Keith Scott Morton
	Jessie Walker	57	Paul Kopelow
	(below)		(above)
20	Jessie Walker		Chris Mead
21	Jessie Walker		(below left)
22	George Ross		Paul Kopelow
23	Keith Scott Morton		(below right)
24	Rick Patrick	58	Chris Mead
	(above)	60	Jessie Walker
	Jessie Walker	62	Ralph Bogertman
	(below)		(left)
25	Keith Scott Morton		Keith Scott Morton
	(above)		(right)
	André Gillardin	63	Jessie Walker
	(below)	64	Keith Scott Morton
26	Paul Kopelow		(above and below)
27	Paul Kopelow (all)	65	Ralph Bogertman
28	Doug Kennedy	66	Keith Scott Morton
29	Keith Scott Morton		(above)
30	Doug Kennedy		Paul Kopelow
31	Keith Scott Morton		(below)
	(left)	67	Keith Scott Morton
	Joshua Green		(left and right)
	(right)	68	James Levin
		69	Jeff McNamara

70 Keith Scott Morton
71 Keith Scott Morton (above and below)
72–73 Keith Scott Morton (left and right)
74 Keith Scott Morton
75 Jessie Walker
76 Jon Elliott
77 Keith Scott Morton
79 Joshua Greene (above)
   Jessie Walker (below)
80 Keith Scott Morton
82 Jon Elliott
83 Jessie Walker (above)
   Keith Scott Morton (below)
85 Jessie Walker
86 Paul Kopelow (left)
   Keith Scott Morton (right)
87 Jessie Walker
90 Keith Scott Morton (left)
   Jessie Walker (center and right)
91 Keith Scott Morton
92 Paul Kopelow (left)
   Keith Scott Morton (right)
93 Jessie Walker (above)
   Keith Scott Morton (below)
94 Keith Scott Morton
95 Paul Kopelow
96 Keith Scott Morton
97 Keith Scott Morton (left and right)
98 Jessie Walker (left)
   Jon Elliott (right)
99 Jessie Walker
100 H. Durston Saylor (above)
   Joshua Greene (below)
101 Joshua Greene
102–103 Joshua Greene

106 Keith Scott Morton
107 Keith Scott Morton (left)
   Joshua Greene (right)
108 Paul Kopelow (all)
109 Jessie Walker
110–111 André Gillardin
113 Keith Scott Morton
114 Keith Scott Morton
115 Keith Scott Morton (above)
   James Levin (below left)
   Jessie Walker (below right)
117 Frank W. Ockenfels 3rd
118 Jessie Walker (left and right)
119 Keith Scott Morton
120 Herb Bleiweiss (all)
121 Jessie Walker (above)
   Keith Scott Morton (below)
122 Paul Kopelow
123 Keith Scott Morton
124 André Gillardin (above)
   Keith Scott Morton (below)
125 Keith Scott Morton (all)
126 Paul Kopelow
127 Ralph Bogertman (above)
   Keith Scott Morton (below left, center, right)
128 Jessie Walker (above and below)
129 Paul Kopelow
130 Paul Kopelow
131 Paul Kopelow (above and below)
132 Keith Scott Morton
133 Keith Scott Morton

134 Keith Scott Morton (left)
   Paul Kopelow (right)
135 Jessie Walker
137 Ernst Beadle
138 Keith Scott Morton
139 Keith Scott Morton
140–141 Paul Kopelow
144–145 Keith Scott Morton (all)
146 Keith Scott Morton (above)
   Jessie Walker (below left, center, right)
147 Keith Scott Morton
148 Ralph Bogertman
149 Keith Scott Morton (above left and right, below right)
   Jessie Walker (below left)
150 Jessie Walker (left)
   André Gillardin (right)
151 Keith Scott Morton
154 Keith Scott Morton
155 Keith Scott Morton
156 Ralph Bogertman (above)
   Jessie Walker (below)
157 Paul Kopelow (above left)
   Rick Patrick (above right)
   Keith Scott Morton (below)
158 Paul Kopelow
159 Paul Kopelow (above and below)
160–161 Paul Kopelow (left and right)
162 Keith Scott Morton (all)
163 Keith Scott Morton
164–165 Jessie Walker
167 Keith Scott Morton

168 Keith Scott Morton (above and below)
169 Keith Scott Morton (above and below)
172 Jessie Walker
173 Jessie Walker (left)
   Joshua Green (right)
175 Jessie Walker
176 Keith Scott Morton
177 Jon Elliott (above)
   Keith Scott Morton (below)
178 Paul Kopelow (all)
179 Paul Kopelow
180 Keith Scott Morton (above)
   Jessie Walker (below)
181 Keith Scott Morton
183 Jon Elliott
186 Jessie Walker (above and below)
187 Jessie Walker
192 Paul Kopelow

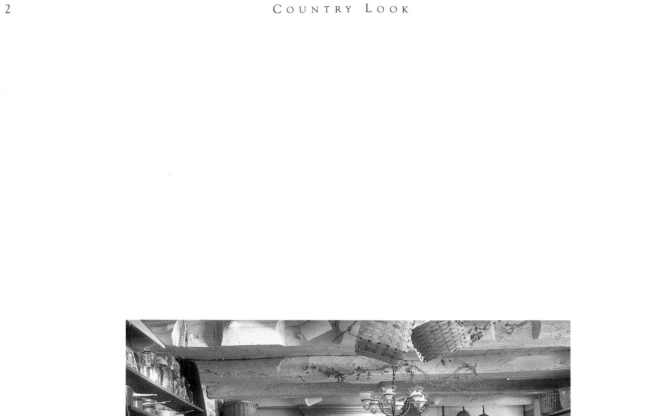